P9-CSS-198

HEADLINE SERIES

No. 315   FOREIGN POLICY ASSOCIATION   Summer

The Persian Gulf in Transition

by Lawrence G. Potter

Cover Design: Ed Bohon $5.95

The Author

LAWRENCE G. POTTER is deputy director of the Gulf/2000 Project and adjunct assistant professor of international affairs at Columbia University. He holds a Ph.D. in history from Columbia and served as senior editor at the Foreign Policy Association from 1984 to 1992. He specializes in Iranian history and U.S. policy toward the Middle East. He is coeditor with Gary Sick of *The Persian Gulf at the Millennium: Essays in Politics, Economy, Security and Religion*, published in September 1997.

The Foreign Policy Association

The Foreign Policy Association is a private, nonprofit, nonpartisan educational organization. Its purpose is to stimulate wider interest and more effective participation in, and greater understanding of, world affairs among American citizens. Among its activities is the continuous publication, dating from 1935, of the HEADLINE SERIES. The author is responsible for factual accuracy and for the views expressed. FPA itself takes no position on issues of U.S. foreign policy.

HEADLINE SERIES (ISSN 0017-8780) is published four times a year, Spring, Summer, Fall and Winter, by the Foreign Policy Association, Inc., 470 Park Avenue So., New York, NY 10016. Chairman, Paul B. Ford; President, Noel V. Lateef; Editor in Chief, Nancy Hoepli-Phalon; Senior Editors, Ann R. Monjo and K.M. Rohan; Assistant Editor, Nicholas Barratt. Subscription rates, $20.00 for 4 issues; $35.00 for 8 issues; $50.00 for 12 issues. Single copy price $5.95; double issue $11.25. Discount 25% on 10 to 99 copies; 30% on 100 to 499; 35% on 500 and over. Payment must accompany all orders. Postage and handling: $2.50 for first copy; $.50 each additional copy. Second-class postage paid at New York, NY, and additional mailing offices. POSTMASTER: Send address changes to HEADLINE SERIES, Foreign Policy Association, 470 Park Avenue So., New York, NY 10016. Copyright 1998 by Foreign Policy Association, Inc. Design by K.M. Rohan. Printed at Science Press, Ephrata, Pennsylvania. Summer 1996. Published January 1998.

Library of Congress Catalog Card No. 97-77153
ISBN 0-87124-179-X

Introduction

THE LAST FOUR U.S. Administrations have proclaimed the Persian Gulf and its vast reserves of oil and natural gas vital to U.S. interests. One fifth of America's oil imports now come from the Gulf, with around 15 percent from Saudi Arabia alone. In defense of these interests, President George Bush sent half a million troops to the region in 1990 and 1991 to terminate Iraq's occupation of Kuwait. Since then, the Clinton Administration has maintained a significant military presence in the Gulf. Although oil is the principal reason for the U.S. presence, the Persian Gulf states also figure in a number of other American foreign policy concerns, including the Arab-Israeli peace process, the growth of political Islam, terrorism, the conventional arms race and the spread of weapons of mass destruction.

The United States today is the predominant external power in the Gulf. In order to maintain its primacy, the United States seeks to constrain Iran and Iraq, which it has labeled outlaw states bent on establishing regional hegemony, and to cooperate closely with friendly Arab governments, especially the six Gulf Cooperation Council (GCC) states: Bahrain, Kuwait, Oman, Qatar, Saudi Arabia and the United Arab Emirates (UAE). The Gulf monarchies' ties to the United States, however, have subjected them to criticism by their own citizens and invigorated the Islamic opposition. In Bahrain, the regional

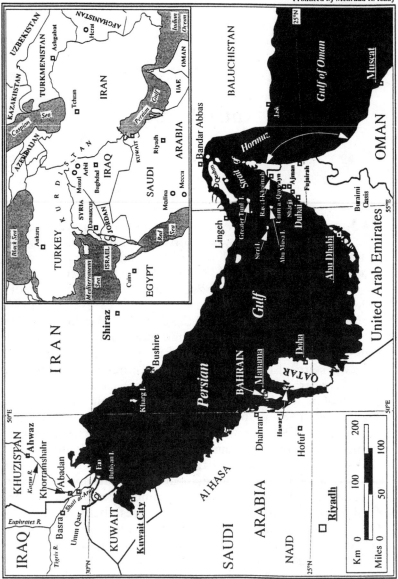

Produced by Mehrdad R. Izady

headquarters of U.S. naval forces, serious antigovernment uprisings have been under way since 1994. Relations with Saudi Arabia, the closest U.S. ally in the region, are uneasy. In 1995 and 1996, terrorists mounted attacks on American servicemen stationed there.

Tensions in the Gulf today are dangerously high, as the world was reminded during the tense three-week standoff between Iraq and UN weapons inspectors in November 1997. Such tensions are reflected in burgeoning arms sales to the region. Since the Iraqi invasion of Kuwait, U.S. firms alone have signed weapons contracts worth $36 billion with the GCC states. In Iraq, President Saddam Hussein's eight-year war with Iran and invasion of Kuwait have impoverished his country and fostered continuing instability. The atmosphere in Iran, and relations between Iran and the GCC countries, improved after the surprise election of moderate Mohammad Khatami as president in May 1997. Yet disillusionment with the legacy of the Iranian revolution of 1978–79, which swept out the shah and established an Islamic republic, is widespread. Khatami must still contend with powerful conservative forces. A number of regional boundary disputes remain unsettled and could flare up at any time. Trust between neighboring states—a prerequisite for defusing problems—is lacking.

The Gulf is a region of strong enemies, weak friends and vital interests. Without U.S. protection, the Gulf monarchies would be vulnerable to pressure from Iran and Iraq. At the same time, U.S. military actions, threatened or actual, against the two "rogue states" could subject the GCC states to reprisals. "If war erupts in this region, people in New York, Baltimore and Indiana will still go on with their way of life, but we will not," cautions Abdullah al-Nafisi, a Kuwaiti political scientist. "The Iranians would not bomb Americans. They would bomb us. We are squeezed in the middle. We have a lot to lose."

Role of the United States

Given its dependence on the Gulf's energy reserves, what alternative does the United States have to protecting its interests there? Is the U.S. commitment to defend the monarchs from external aggression becoming a liability to them? Will adverse events within the region, or domestic public opinion, lead to a withdrawal of U.S. forces? American troops in Saudi Arabia believe they are being regularly "stalked" by terrorist groups waiting for an opportunity to strike. In the UAE, where an estimated 240 American ships made port calls in 1997, tens of thousands of U.S. troops are granted shore leave annually and both countries fear it is only a matter of time before a serious incident takes place.

In the wake of the bombings in Saudi Arabia in 1996, the U.S. ambassador to Kuwait, Ryan Crocker, maintained that "there will be no diminishing, no withdrawal, no reduction of U.S. military elements or units in this area." But the Defense Department began to cut back the number of U.S. military families in Kuwait and relocated over 4,000 American troops in Saudi Arabia to a remote, more defensible area. Prince Bandar ibn Sultan, the Saudi ambassador to Washington, said in February 1997 that the U.S. troop presence in the Gulf was temporary and could end once Saddam Hussein leaves power. The following month, a report issued by Republican members of the Senate Appropriations Committee criticized the expense of maintaining U.S. forces on a long-term war footing in the Gulf.

Is current U.S. policy in tune with American needs and regional realities? European and Arab support for continuing the sanctions imposed by the United Nations against Iraq after the Persian Gulf war is faltering, and there is growing apprehension that Saddam Hussein may remain in power for some time. In a blatant challenge to the U.S. trade sanctions against Iran, in September 1997 the French energy company Total, in conjunction with Russia's Gazprom and the Malaysian state oil firm Petronas, signed a $2 billion deal with Iran to develop a major gas field in the Persian Gulf. Members of a group of Gulf experts convened by the Stanley Foundation of Muscatine, Iowa, in October 1996 concluded that "a U.S. policy committed to the preservation of the status quo is a policy certain to fail. The countries of the Persian Gulf region, without exception, are in the process of fundamental political, social, and economic change. The United States must be flexible enough to anticipate and adapt to changing circumstances when necessary, and to help channel that change in constructive ways when possible."

President Bill Clinton declared the election of President Khatami in Iran an "interesting" and "hopeful" development and hinted at the possibility of some future reconciliation. "I have never been pleased about the estrangements between the people of the United States and the people of Iran," Clinton said. But while Washington awaits evidence that Iran has changed its attitude toward "the Great Satan," U.S. policy remains unchanged.

American policy is built on the premise that the main threat to the GCC countries is external aggression. But what about the internal threat, from citizens dissatisfied with their exclusion from the political process, with restraints on free expression and with the lack of economic progress? What role can the United States play to combat these sources of instability? Should it urge its allies to implement political and economic reforms and show greater respect for human rights? Should it continue to sell arms to the Gulf states—arms they cannot really afford, which lead to greater danger of war? Finally, should the United States continue to assume principal responsibility for the security of the Gulf, when allies in Europe and Japan are much more dependent upon its oil? The United States presently maintains 20,000 troops and 20 warships in the Gulf at a cost of $30 billion to $60 billion annually, according to Graham E. Fuller, a senior political analyst at the Rand Corporation. It is not known how long U.S. forces will be welcome in the Gulf countries.

Profile of the Persian Gulf

The Persian Gulf is a 600-mile-long arm of the Indian Ocean, which separates the Arabian peninsula from Iran. (Since the 1960s some Arab states have referred to the Persian Gulf as the

The Persian Gulf States

Bob Mansfield

	Area (sq. miles)	Population (millions, mid-1997)	Annual Pop. Growth Rate %	GNP Per Capita ($U.S., 1995)	Oil Reserves (billion barrels)	Oil Production (barrels per day, 1996)
Bahrain	239	0.6 [a]	2.0 [b]	7,840	.21	103,800
Iran	631,660	67.5 [c]	2.7 [d]	see note [e]	93	3,675,300
Iraq	168,751	21.2	2.8	—	112	600,000
Kuwait	6,880	1.8	2.2	17,390	94	1,817,500
Oman	120,861	2.3	3.4	4,820	5.1	882,500
Qatar	4,247	0.6	1.7	11,600 [f]	3.7	479,800
Saudi Arabia	754,258	19.5 [g]	3.1	7,040	259	7,841,000
UAE	27,188	2.3 [h]	1.8	17,400 [i]	97.8	2,216,800

Sources: Area from *Atlas of the Middle East* (Central Intelligence Agency, 1993); population figures, growth rates and GNP per capita from *1997 World Population Data Sheet* (Population Reference Bureau, 1997); oil reserve and production figures from *Oil and Gas Journal DataLook*, 1997.

Notes: a. & b. Bahrain government estimates are 620,378 (mid-1997) and a 3.6% growth rate in 1996. c. & d. According to the Iranian census, population in 1996 was 60 million and the growth rate, 1.6%. Latter is far below outside estimates, resulting in lower population total. e. Per capita income estimates vary from $5,766 (UNDP estimate based on purchasing power) down to $1,200-$1,500, according to experts in Iran, depending on exchange rate used. f. Per capita income of Qatari nationals is $22,000, according to Reuters. g. According to official Saudi figures, the population in 1997 was 16,948,388, including 4,638,335 foreign residents. h. & i. Official UAE figures estimate population at 2.4 million at end of 1996 and per capita income at $16,500 in 1995.

Arabian Gulf, in an attempt to give it a new identity and belittle Iran.) The Gulf is surrounded by Iran, the predominant state in terms of population, and seven Arab countries: Iraq, Kuwait, Saudi Arabia, Bahrain, Qatar, the UAE and Oman. The Gulf is bounded by the Shatt al-Arab waterway in the north, which forms the frontier between Iran and Iraq, and the Strait of Hormuz in the south, which connects it to the Gulf of Oman and the Indian Ocean. The strait, which is 34 miles wide at its narrowest point, is the choke point of the Gulf: some 30,000 vessels, mostly oil tankers, pass through it each year. The possibility of its closure by Iran has long been a nightmare for Western oil importers and defense planners.

The Gulf states contain some 116 million people, representing many ethnic, religious, linguistic and political communities. A major cleavage pits Arab against Persian. Arabic, a Semitic language, is spoken in Iraq and the countries of the peninsula, whereas Iran has an Aryan heritage, and its main language, Persian (Farsi), is an Indo-European tongue. Persians regard their cultural legacy as richer than that of the Arabs, although their religion, Islam, was founded by an Arab, the Prophet Muhammad.

Muslims (followers of the Islamic religion) are split into two major sects, Sunni and Shiites. The two differ over who was legitimately entitled to lead the Islamic community after the death of Muhammad in A.D. 632. The Sunnis, who predominate, believe that the community should choose its own leader. Shiites, who are a majority in Iran, believe leadership is vested in the family of the Prophet. Sunni Islam has historically been associated with bestowing legitimacy on the power of rulers; Shiite Islam, with opposition, martyrdom and revolt.

The present importance of the Gulf stems from its energy deposits. Sixty-five percent of the world's known oil reserves are located in the Gulf countries, which produce over a third of the world's daily output. (By comparison, North America holds 8.5 percent of the world's reserves.) Saudi Arabia ranks first in reserves, with 259 billion barrels, followed by Iraq (112 billion), the UAE (98 billion), Kuwait (94 billion), and Iran (93 billion).

The cost of oil production in the Gulf is the lowest in the world: it currently ranges from fifty cents a barrel in Saudi Arabia to $2 in offshore wells in the UAE. The Gulf is also rich in natural gas, with Iran and Qatar holding the world's second- and third-largest reserves, respectively.

In the future, the vast oil and gas reserves of the Caspian basin (believed to hold up to 200 billion barrels) will rival those of the Gulf in importance. Rising energy demand in China, Japan and South Asia has led the new republics of Azerbaijan, Kazakhstan and Turkmenistan to seek Western help in developing and exporting these resources. American oil companies have so far been hindered in the new oil rush in Central Asia because the U.S. government will not permit them to participate in the construction of pipelines across Iran, the shortest export route. As a consequence, Russian and Asian oil companies are in a strong position to exploit Caspian energy reserves in the future.

The Gulf in History

"The Gulf is not oil. The Gulf is its people and its land," Kuwaiti historian Muhammad Rumaihi reminds readers. "So it was before the discovery of oil, and so it will remain when the oil disappears. Oil is no more than a historical phase in this part of the Arab world—and a rather short one at that."

Before the discovery of oil, the Gulf was a backwater noted mainly for its infernal climate. Sir Arnold Wilson, a British colonial administrator with long experience there, wrote in 1928:

A certain aroma of romance hangs round the name of the Persian Gulf, but those who know the region best are probably least disposed to regard it in a romantic light. It is an area of bleak coasts, torrid winds, and pitiless sunshine. The amenities of life are few and far between. Nature is in her fiercest humor and man has done little to improve upon her handiwork. The population is scanty, the standard of living low. Towns are few and insanitary; villages little more than clusters of mud huts. To a casual visitor it might seem a mere backwater to which civilization has scarcely penetrated.

10

The modern strategic importance of the Gulf dates from the mid-nineteenth century, when three great empires confronted each other there: British India, czarist Russia and Ottoman Turkey. The British established political control over much of the Gulf in the early 1800s and kept it for 150 years. A tradition of outside involvement persists today.

After World War I, the political map of much of the Middle East was redrawn. The Ottoman Empire was replaced by modern nations, including Turkey, Iraq and Saudi Arabia. The small Arab shaikhdoms on the western shore of the Gulf were under British protection until 1971 (in the case of Kuwait, 1961). Iran was never a colony, and for much of the nineteenth and twentieth centuries Britain competed with Russia for influence there.

The oil revenues that began to accumulate after World War II enabled the Gulf states to modernize, and, by the 1960s and 1970s, to provide generous entitlement programs for their citizens. The state became what political scientists call a "rentier" one: the income from oil accrued directly to the ruler, who provided for his citizens' economic security in return for their political loyalty. This arrangement bought time for the tribal shaikhs who had been in power before the discovery of oil. It also led to the growth of a "rentier mentality" among the citizenry, who felt a sense of entitlement to riches, whether they worked or not.

Domestic Challenges

All of the Gulf states must contend with rapidly rising populations. In 1950, their combined population was estimated to be some 24 million; today, it is around 116 million and is projected to rise to 209 million by the year 2025. In Iran, a population of 35 million at the time of the revolution in 1978 had swollen to 60 million by 1996. The rate of population growth, however, has not been accompanied by an equivalent rise in oil revenues, the main source of government income. Today, the oil monarchies can no longer afford the generous social programs they instituted in wealthier days. Unemployment is now a widespread problem, and millions of jobs must be created in the next 15 years. At the same time that countries cut benefits, they are confronted with demands for more say in government.

The holiday from reality is over in the Gulf monarchies, both politically and economically, according to oil economist Vahan Zanoyan. To survive, the governments must forge a new social contract that allows for greater political participation. The question is whether the rulers are willing to make the changes needed, especially if their monopoly of power is threatened. It is not clear that Gulf monarchies are ready to confront their problems: "Surprisingly little indigenous discussion takes place regarding the future of the area," according to scholar Anwar Gargash of the UAE. "No regionwide consensus or outlook is emerging, and no Gulf perspective is crystallizing regarding the future state of affairs."

◄◊

In order to create a better understanding of this critical region and the future challenges it faces, this HEADLINE SERIES will briefly review the historical legacy; the transformation of traditional societies into modern states following the discovery of oil; the significance of the two major wars in the Gulf in the 1980s and 1990s; and the structural problems facing the Gulf countries now and in the coming years. A final chapter will discuss U.S. policy toward the region.

◊►

For basic information on the Persian Gulf states, the U.S. State Department's **Background** **Notes** *on individual countries are available on the Internet, at*

http://www.state.gov/www/background_notes/index.html

1

From Traditional to Modern States

THE PERSIAN GULF, an important trade route connecting the Middle East to Africa, India and China, has its own distinct cultural identity. The Gulf has historically been an integrated region, with the constant exchange of people, commerce and religious movements. Before the modern era, peoples of the region shared a maritime culture based on pearling, fishing and long-distance trade, and many tribes moved about freely. This led to an intermingling of ethnic, linguistic and religious communities, with many Arabic speakers and Sunni Muslims on the Persian side of the Gulf and a number of Shiites (some Persian-speaking) on the Arab side.

Because of physical barriers—principally mountains and deserts—peoples living on the shores of the Gulf had closer relations with each other than with those living in the interior. In the nineteenth century, they had little contact with the primary regional powers, the Persian and the Ottoman empires and the shaikhs in Arabia, all of whom had capitals inland. The population in the coastal towns was part of an interlinked system that included agricultural villages and oases that sustained the caravan trade.

Maritime Society in the Gulf

The Persian Gulf's orientation was toward the ocean, and its seamen maintained close ties with the Indian subcontinent and East Africa. A well-organized Arab dhow (sailing vessel) trade frequented ports along these coasts: ships would load up with dates from Basra, in southern Iraq, and sail down to Africa in the fall on the northeast monsoon, peddling the dates and whatever else they could trade, such as salt and rice. They returned on the southwest monsoon with mangrove poles from Africa for construction and teak, coir (coarse coconut fiber) and shipbuilding materials from India. In addition to their cargoes, the dhows were always packed with passengers, including pilgrims to the holy cities of Mecca and Medina in Saudi Arabia. Dhow transport was very cheap (the sailors received no pay, only a share in the meager profits), perfectly suited to the climate, and provided storage at the destination until the dates could be sold. As recently as the eve of World War II, an estimated 2,000 vessels with 30,000 to 40,000 sailors engaged in such trade in the ports of the Arabian peninsula.

During the summer months, when the dhows could not sail south because of adverse winds, the pearl beds, the most valuable resource of the Gulf before the discovery of oil, were the centers of activity. Pearling was very much a seasonal occupation, taking place from June through September when the surface temperature of the water was around 85°F. Although pearls were found throughout much of the Gulf, the best ones were taken from waters northeast of Bahrain. Most were sold in Bombay, India. With the introduction of Japanese cultured pearls in the 1930s, the bottom dropped out of the market, and many of the former pearlers went to work in the young oil industry.

14

A dhow—a traditional sailing vessel that has been used for centuries to transport goods and passengers in Persian Gulf waters—in the harbor at Abadan, Iran.

UPI/Corbis-Bettmann

Tribes and State Formation

In addition to a maritime heritage, the peoples on the Gulf's southern shore also share a legacy of tribal rule that originated in the interior of Arabia, where pastoral nomads were constantly migrating to sustain themselves and their herds of camels, sheep and goats. (In contrast to the Bedouins of Arabia, Iranian tribes usually migrated to the highlands in summer and wintered near the Gulf.) Anthropologists have not been able to agree on a definition of "tribe," and tribal people tend to view themselves very differently than outsiders do, especially governments. Kinship and patrilineal descent, real or imagined, are usually important aspects of a tribe's social structure. The power, cohesion and even identity of a tribe can change, with new tribes being formed and older ones disintegrating.

Traditionally, tribal leadership was vested in a shaikh, but his authority was only that of first among equals. The shaikh's authority was provisional, and dissatisfied tribesmen could overthrow or assassinate him. (In the nineteenth century, ruling shaikhs in the Gulf were frequently overthrown.) It was not unusual for populations unhappy with a shaikh to move elsewhere en masse. For example, in 1909 a group of pearl merchants in Kuwait, objecting to new taxes imposed by the ruler, took up residence in Bahrain in protest. The shaikh gave in and canceled the taxes, since he could not do without the revenues from the merchants.

Typical tribal institutions were the *majlis,* or public audience, where anyone could approach the ruler to seek redress of his problems, and the process of *shura,* or consultation. In a consultative form of government, the leading shaikh ruled with the cooperation of his kinsmen and prominent merchants. If one shaikh was overthrown, another member of his family often assumed power, for legitimacy to rule was reckoned to run in families.

Tribes were the key to forming modern states in the Arabian peninsula; and, in fact, all of the current ruling dynasties are of tribal origin. The religious reform movement known as Wahhabism, which arose in the central region of Najd, Saudi Arabia, in the eighteenth century, has also played an important role in politically unifying the peninsula. The Wahhabi version of Islam is austere: it seeks a return to a purified faith and opposes all "innovations," such as saint-worship and Shiism. It was founded by Muhammad b. Abd al-Wahhab (d.1791), a preacher who formed a partnership in 1744 with a local chieftain, Muhammad b. Saud (d. 1765), and went on to conquer much of the peninsula.

Possibly because of drought in the interior, many tribes in the eighteenth century moved to the Gulf coast. The Al Sabah family established itself in Kuwait, the Al Khalifa in Bahrain, and the Al Thani in Qatar a century later. The migration to the coast and the growth of towns, such as Kuwait, Bahrain, Abu Dhabi and Dubai, marked an important development in Gulf society. It led to the stronger identification of a tribe with a particular geographical location and helped to strengthen the authority of the ruler. The precarious balance of power between the nomadic Bedouins and the settled communities began to shift in favor of the latter. Increased urbanization also led to greater contact with the outside world. The British did not suppress tribalism in the Gulf but they profoundly altered its character by giving the shaikhs under their protection the means to exert more autocratic control.

British Paramountcy

European powers' intervention in the Gulf, starting in the early 1800s, decisively influenced the political evolution of the Gulf states. The maritime warfare (characterized as "piracy" by Europeans) that flourished in the Gulf was a menace to their trade and communications, and the African slave trade was an affront to their sensibilities. The British interest, which at first was primarily commercial, was increasingly bound up with concern for the defense of India and subsequently a determination to exclude other powers, especially Russia.

Imperial policy toward the Gulf was formulated by authorities in both Britain and British India, which often resulted in confusion. The Foreign Office in London was chiefly concerned with maintaining its European alliances and not provoking Russia and the Ottomans. The India Office, which represented authorities in Bombay and Calcutta, resented being obliged to subsidize Gulf security while often being overruled on policy. British diplomats assigned to the Gulf were members of the Indian Political Service. Britain's policy in the Gulf did not unfold according to a grand plan but, due to the slowness of communications, was often the result of actions taken by local officials that their government later had to support.

Britain initially brought peace to the waters of the Gulf by establishing what became known as the trucial system. In 1835, it persuaded the shaikhs in the lower Gulf to sign a treaty promising to abstain from warfare during the pearling season. Any infraction was to be punished by the British Navy. This treaty worked well, and was renewed annually, becoming permanent in 1853. The so-called Pirate Coast was now referred to as the Trucial Coast, the area that today comprises the UAE.

Britain wanted to avoid establishing formal protectorates in the Gulf; it could not afford them and did not want to get bogged down in regulating the internal affairs of littoral states. In 1861, however, it recognized the independence of Bahrain and pledged to protect it from attack. (Since Bahrain was an island, the British navy could ensure its security.) Later Britain concluded a number of exclusive agreements with other Gulf shaikhs, assuring them protection in return for control over their foreign policy. British dominance of the Gulf in the last quarter of the nineteenth century was challenged by the Ottomans, who occupied the Al Hasa region on the Arabian coast south of Kuwait in 1871 and stationed a garrison in Doha; by the French, who sought influence in Oman; by the Germans, who sought to build a railway to Kuwait; and by the Russians, who already exercised influence on the Persian government.

In 1891, Britain entered into an exclusive agreement with the sultan of Muscat and Oman. The ruler agreed (in a "nonalienation clause") not to cede, sell or mortgage any portion of his territory to any foreign power except Britain. The following year, Britain signed similar agreements with the Trucial shaikhs, who further promised not to permit another power, without British permission, to station a diplomat on their territory. Qatar was brought into this system in 1916.

For most of the nineteenth century, the British considered Kuwait a dependency of the Ottomans. The latter's influence increased after they invaded Al Hasa, and the ruling shaikh of Kuwait rendered a nominal tribute to them and accepted an Ottoman title. However, the Ottoman government in Basra did not intervene in Kuwaiti affairs. In 1896, the ruler was murdered by his half-brother, Shaikh Mubarak, who seized power and appealed to the British for protection. In 1899 Britain agreed to guarantee his rule and that of his descendants in return for a nonalienation clause and the control of foreign relations. In an unratified accord of 1913, the British recognized Kuwait (defined to include Bubiyan and Warba islands) as an autonomous district of the Ottoman Empire, while the Ottomans accepted the 1899 agreement, including British control of Kuwait's foreign relations. At the outbreak of World War I in 1914, Kuwait became an independent state under British protection.

The circumstances under which Shaikh Mubarak exercised power illustrate how the British changed the nature of shaikhly authority. After Britain pledged to support him, Mubarak built a new palace, bought a yacht and an automobile, and raised his salute from five guns to twelve—one less than the British Resident. In a similar manner, shaikhs throughout the Gulf, who had previously ruled in consultation with their tribesmen and the merchants, became increasingly autocratic. The British treated the shaikhs they dealt with as rulers *(hakim)* over the settled urban populations—which exceeded the prerogatives of a shaikh as traditionally understood—and held them accountable for the actions of their inhabitants. Upon independence, they would assume the grander title of *amir*, often used for military commanders and princes.

By curtailing smuggling and the profitable slave and arms trade, the British also altered the traditional economy of the Gulf. European steamships provided regular service between Bombay and the Gulf ports after 1862, and the opening of the Suez Canal in 1869 led to more frequent service with Europe. Europeans took over most of the long-distance trade (which increased the importance of a few ports such as Basra (in Iraq), and Bushire and Mohammera (in Iran), while relegating native dhows to the peddlar trade in smaller ports. Local businessmen now became agents for goods manufactured in Europe as the Gulf became increasingly integrated into the world economy.

Boundary Drawing and the Question of Borders

The dissolution of the Ottoman Empire after World War I put the victors, principally Britain and France, in charge of dividing up the former enemy territories. The Persian boundaries had been largely settled before the war, but there was no agreement on the exact boundaries in the Arabian peninsula.

Part of the problem was conceptual: linking sovereignty to territory was a European idea. In Arabia, traditionally, people were loyal to a leader, not to a geographic entity. A shaikh held sovereignty over his tribe, wherever they roamed throughout their *dirah*, or grazing area. A tribe's location could change depending on the climate, and no arbitrary boundary in the desert could constrain its migrations.

With the establishment of Iraq as a British mandate in 1920, the British had to draw a border separating it from the Saudi region of Najd and Kuwait. The new boundary left Iraq with only 36 miles of frontage on the Persian Gulf, and its main port of Basra, located 75 miles upriver, was the only outlet for a virtually landlocked country. Kuwait, on the other hand, had one of the best harbors on the Gulf and 310 miles of coastline. Moreover, Iraqi vessels had to pass by or through Kuwaiti waters near the islands of Bubiyan and Warba in order to reach their small port of Umm Qasr. Since the late 1930s, Iraq has tried to acquire these islands, for without them it will never feel secure about its access to the Gulf.

There has also been a long-standing dispute between Iran and Iraq over the Shatt al-Arab, the waterway formed by the confluence of the Tigris, Euphrates and Karun rivers that serves as their common border. Under an 1847 treaty that was reaffirmed in 1937, the entire waterway up to the Iranian shore (except for a short stretch opposite Abadan, Iran) was considered Iraqi territory. Iran, however, has insisted that its territory extends to the deepest navigable channel, or *thalweg*, in effect dividing sovereignty over the river between the two states.

One of the most serious flash points in the Gulf today, the dispute over the sovereignty of Abu Musa and the Tunb islands, also originated in the late nineteenth century. Their value is primarily strategic: they are located in the shipping lanes near the Strait of Hormuz. Proof of ownership of the islands before the nineteenth century is inconclusive, but by the late 1800s, Persia had laid claim to all of them on the basis that it had owned them before the British arrived and that in the 1880s Greater Tunb island had paid taxes to Persia.

However, the Arab rulers of Sharja and Ras al-Khaimah (both now part of the UAE) claimed Abu Musa and the Tunbs, respectively. They were backed by the British government, which preferred to have the islands controlled by shaikhs under its influence rather than by Persia. In 1971, as the British withdrew from the Gulf, Iran seized the Tunbs and forced Sharja to accept an Iranian garrison on Abu Musa. Iran regarded itself entitled to the islands since it had already made a concession to the Arab states by relinquishing its claim to Bahrain in 1970.

Oil and Social Change

The story of the Persian Gulf in the twentieth century is the story of oil—the exploration, discovery and export of petroleum—and the effect this has had on traditional societies. The vast revenues that suddenly accrued to the fortunate Gulf states led to far-reaching economic changes, but on the Arabian peninsula, few political ones. Indeed, the oil revenues, coupled with British support, enabled monarchies, which were overthrown in most other Middle Eastern states after World War II, to survive and thrive in the Gulf.

Oil was first discovered in southwest Iran in 1908. In 1914, on the eve of World War I, the British government, which needed oil for its warships, assumed control of the producers, the Anglo-Persian Oil Company. Oil was discovered in commercial quantities in Iraq in the Kurdish region in 1927, in Bahrain in 1932, and in Saudi Arabia and Kuwait in 1938. Before World War II, Iran was the leading oil exporter in the Middle East, and its refinery at Abadan was the largest in the world.

Oil operations in a country were usually controlled exclusively by a single company, often a joint venture or partnership. Such an arrangement discouraged competition and prevented overproduction, which would lower prices. Britain initially tried to prevent the Gulf shaikhs from signing agreements with non-British companies, but eventually American firms won concessions in Bahrain, Kuwait and Saudi Arabia. The

British refused the United States permission to open any consulates in the area, however, until 1950, when the first one opened in Kuwait.

The most famous petroleum partnership was the Arabian-American Oil Company, known as Aramco, which was granted a concession by King Ibn Saud in 1933. "If the first pillar of the Saudi state has been the Wahhabi religious movement," writes historian J.B. Kelly, "the second has been the Arabian-American Oil Company....The company has served the house of Saud as guide, confidant, tutor, counselor, emissary, advocate, steward and factotum." Aramco aimed to be a model company, not only seeing to the training, health care and housing of its workers, but also building roads, hospitals and water pipelines for the surrounding community. Its expatriate workers were housed in enclaves that resembled suburban America.

After World War II, major changes took place in the oil industry. Iran had long complained that Britain was too stingy in the compensation it paid: in 1950, the oil company paid Iran £16 million in royalties and made £100 million in profits from its Iranian operations. When Aramco agreed in 1950 to share profits with Saudi Arabia on a 50-50 basis, Iran wanted a similar agreement. The (now renamed) Anglo-Iranian Oil Company, however, would not agree to profit sharing. Matters came to a head when Iran's prime minister, Mohammad Mossadeq (1951–53), nationalized the company. For Britain, this was a great humiliation and meant the loss of a key economic asset. Mossadeq's government was overthrown in August 1953 and the shah, Mohammad Reza Pahlavi, was restored to power in a countercoup that was organized by U.S. and British intelligence.

Thereafter, although Iran retained sovereignty over its oil, it struck a new agreement with a consortium of oil companies to operate the concession. The British share was reduced to 40 percent and American companies received an equal stake. (It was not until 1973 that Iran took full control of its oil operations.) A major consequence of the Iranian crisis was that companies across the Gulf, especially in Kuwait and Saudi Arabia, stepped up production. At the same time new commercial quantities of oil were discovered—in Qatar and Abu Dhabi in 1960, in Oman in 1963, and in Dubai in 1969.

The Impact of Oil

The development of the oil industry set in motion many changes. Between World Wars I and II, it began to open up the Gulf to the outside world at the expense of British control. For the first time, local rulers struck commercial deals with oil companies and gained a secure source of income independent of any British subsidy.

The Gulf area was also becoming more important as an international communications and transportation hub, with British airlines securing landing rights to stop over on the way to India. (Traditional ties with the subcontinent, though, were becoming less important than relations with the greater Arab world.) With increased oil exploration came more pressure to delineate boundaries. This led, after World War II, to the protracted Buraimi oasis dispute between Saudi Arabia (backed by the United States) and Oman and Abu Dhabi (backed by Britain) over boundaries in the southeastern part of the Arabian peninsula, which was believed to contain oil. In 1952, Saudi troops occupied part of the oasis. Arbitration failed, and in 1955 the Saudis were evicted by forces from Abu Dhabi and Oman under British command. Not until 1974 did Saudi Arabia relinquish its claim, in return for a strip of territory giving it access to the Gulf east of Qatar.

Oil proved to be a mixed blessing. It provided salvation to Bahrain in the 1930s, when the economy collapsed along with the pearl industry. In the postwar period, it paid for the rapid modernization of Iran and the Arab monarchies, some of which enjoyed very high per capita incomes. In the 1960s and 1970s, the Arab Gulf states began providing their people free education, health care and housing. But there was also a downside. Even the shah of Iran, in a 1973 interview with the Italian journalist Oriana Fallaci, was ambivalent about the value of Iran's great resource: "So much has been written about the curse we call oil, and believe me, when you have it, on the one hand it's a blessing but on the other it's a great inconvenience. Because it represents such a danger. The world could blow up on account of this damned oil."

The modernization process, which lasted for centuries in the West, has been compressed into decades in the Gulf countries, putting a great strain on traditional societies. Saudi Arabian novelist Abdelrahman Munif, in the first volume of a monumental trilogy in Arabic entitled *Cities of Salt,* describes a Bedouin village's tragic encounter with American oil prospectors. The author's theme is that the discovery of oil was a curse: the desire for material gain replaced old values of loyalty, honor and respect for tradition. "The tragedy is not in our having the oil," he said in an interview, "but in the way we use the wealth it has created and in the future awaiting us after it has run out." The availability of huge oil revenues, he believes, corrupted political leaders and turned Saudi Arabia into a repressive state.

Legitimacy to Rule

Governments of the states created in the Gulf in the twentieth century—Iraq, Saudi Arabia, Kuwait, Bahrain, Qatar and the UAE—keenly feel the need to create a sense of national identity. Governments of Iraq, for example, have long promoted the idea that ethnic, religious and linguistic differences are irrelevant, since all its citizens are Iraqis. (Some fear that Iraq is now undergoing a process of "retribalization," in which people are returning to primordial loyalties of clan, family and religion.) In the Arabian peninsula, governments have tried to create a historical memory and national symbols to elicit loyalty and reinforce the legitimacy of the rulers. Governments have emphasized their cultural heritage *(turath)* by carrying out archaeological excavations and building new museums in places such as Doha (Qatar) and Dubai (UAE). The challenge in all the Gulf states has been to reconcile traditional forms of rule with modern forms of political expression.

On the Arabian side of the Gulf, Islam and tribalism have traditionally provided legitimacy to the ruling families. In Saudi

Arabia, their close association with Wahhabi Islam has given the Al Saud rulers a status that other Gulf monarchs lack. However, Islam and tribalism, which had previously acted as a check on the rulers, now have been adapted to serve them, according to political scientist F. Gregory Gause III. The rulers have made the clerical establishment dependent upon the state by financing it, something that never happened in Shiite Iran. The tribes are now under effective state control, although the ruler makes a public display of his fidelity to tribal institutions, such as the majlis and shura. "What most Westerners see as a 'traditional' political culture is in fact a construction of recent decades, in which rulers employ a political language redolent of Islamic and tribal overtones to convince their citizens of the legitimacy of their political system," notes Gause.

◦§

Over the past century, the traditional way of life in the Arab Gulf states has been irrevocably changed, due in large measure to the British intervention and the rise of the oil industry. External and internal forces have served to reinforce the power and wealth of one segment of the population, the ruling shaikhs. Because of the way in which the modern states were formed and boundaries arbitrarily delimited, tribal and family loyalties and religious, linguistic and ethnic identities in many cases are more important than country citizenship. These are at the root of many of the present tensions in the region.

2

The Gulf Wars

THE PERSIAN GULF states have been profoundly affected by two recent major conflicts, the Iran-Iraq war of 1980–88 and the Persian Gulf war of 1990–91. The wars were immensely destructive in terms of lives and infrastructure, and they have set back the development of Iran and Iraq by perhaps a decade. They have inflamed tensions and raised the level of distrust among people in the littoral states. The first war carried an undertone of ethnic (Arab vs. Persian) and religious (Sunni vs. Shiite) hostility, whereas the second pitted Arab against Arab, giving the lie to decades of rhetoric about pan-Arab solidarity. Although the hostilities have ended, grievances remain that could explode at some future time.

These wars focused international attention on the Gulf and prompted the United States to an unprecedented level of military involvement in the region. They also led to a rare U.S.-Soviet agreement on policy aims that helped contain the first conflict and end the second.

The Iran-Iraq War

The single most important factor precipitating the Iran-Iraq conflict was the Iranian revolution led by Ayatollah Ruhollah Khomeini. The upheaval in Iran in 1978–79 posed a threat to Iraq, whose government was apprehensive that Khomeini's propaganda would foment unrest among Iraqi Shiites. At the same time it presented an opportunity: if Saddam Hussein could overthrow the new regime, he could prevent the export of the revolution and possibly even annex Khuzistan, Iran's oil-rich southwestern province. Most importantly, Iraq hoped to gain hegemony in the Gulf at Iran's expense.

War with Iran was a calculated risk. But Iraq believed that due to the disorganized state of the Iranian military, its defenses would quickly crumble. In the summer and fall of 1980 the Iranian regime was preoccupied fighting its internal enemies. In addition, there was little likelihood of the superpowers intervening: the United States was trying to arrange the release of its hostages seized in the U.S. embassy in Tehran, the Iranian capital, on November 4, 1979, and the Soviet Union was allied with Iraq.

The stated aims of the war were to obtain Iran's recognition of Iraqi sovereignty over the entire Shatt al-Arab waterway, to make Iran desist from interfering in Iraq's internal affairs and to return the islands of Abu Musa and the Tunbs to the UAE. This last gesture was designed to demonstrate Iraq's role as the protector of the Gulf.

On September 22, 1980, Iraq bombed Tehran and invaded Khuzistan. Saddam Hussein's expectation of an easy victory was soon dashed. Iraqi forces advanced 50 miles but captured only one major city, the port of Khorramshahr. The military initiative then passed to Iran which, in May 1982, liberated Khorramshahr and drove Iraqi troops out of Khuzistan. At this point, Iraq announced it would accept binding arbitration to settle the conflict.

Iran refused. Many Iranians, who referred to the conflict as the "imposed war," were convinced that Iraq attacked it under orders from the United States and with the complicity of the

Soviet Union in order to cause the downfall of the revolutionary government. Before Iran would agree to end the war, it stipulated that Saddam Hussein had to step down, Iraq had to be branded the aggressor by an international tribunal, and Iran had to be guaranteed large reparations. Iraq would also have to take back thousands of ethnic Persians whom it had expelled on security grounds prior to the war. From the outset, there was intense personal hostility between Ayatollah Khomeini and Saddam Hussein.

In addition to ethnic and religious differences, Iran and Iraq had conflicting ideologies—pan-Arabism in the case of Iraq, pan-Islam in the case of Iran. Iraq, governed by a Sunni Arab minority, stressed its ties with other Arab countries and claimed to be guarding the eastern flank of the Arab world against the spread of radical Shiism. Khomeini, on the other hand, believed that Islamic solidarity was more important than nationalism and that Islamic unity took precedence over present-day political frontiers.

Strategies of War

Iran launched a series of annual offensives from 1983 to 1987 to bring down Saddam Hussein's government and liberate pockets of Iranian territory held by Iraq. Iraq's strategy was to squeeze Iran economically and force it to the bargaining table. (Iran was almost wholly dependent on its oil exports through the Gulf for income, whereas Iraq exported most of its own oil via pipeline to the Mediterranean and Red Sea.) Iraq destroyed Iran's refinery at Abadan and repeatedly bombed Iran's main oil-export terminal at Kharg Island in the northern Gulf. It attacked shipping bound for Iran, which responded in kind, and during the "tanker war" that ensued the two countries attacked 543 ships, mostly from neutral nations.

Iran also sought to undermine its neighbor's economy. It formed an alliance with Syria, an Arab state governed by a rival branch of the Baath party, which also held power in Iraq. Iran's strategy was to maintain the offensive, forcing Iraq to keep its troops in a state of readiness along a long frontier, and to refuse to negotiate despite military setbacks. The only Iranian victories were the capture of two small but strategically valuable areas, the Majnun oil fields in February 1984 and the Fao peninsula south of Basra in February 1986. But Iran did not have the logistic capacity or adequate weapons to sustain its offensives for long. Although the fighting continued, Iran's leaders were divided over the wisdom of pursuing a war Tehran could not win and certainly could not afford.

Growing Internationalization

The major regional response to the war was the formation in May 1981 of the Gulf Cooperation Council. The GCC aimed to promote military and political cooperation, but could do little against its two overbearing neighbors. The Gulf monarchs feared from the start that the war could spread, threatening their oil revenues and possibly their governments. Iranian leaders had made it clear that their revolution was suitable for export. The rulers were also troubled by Iraq's intentions, yet felt that they had no choice but to support Saddam Hussein financially. The GCC countries contributed an estimated $35 billion in economic and military "loans" to Iraq with little prospect they would be repaid.

Some of Iran's Arab neighbors suspected it of sabotage and terrorism: they accused it of backing groups that attempted a coup d'état in Bahrain in December 1981 and set off explosions at the American and French embassies in Kuwait in December 1983. In early 1984, Iran warned that if it was prevented from exporting its oil, it would retaliate by closing the Strait of Hormuz. This threat greatly alarmed the West, and President Ronald Reagan vowed to keep the strait open. (Actually, it was too wide and deep to block physically, but the United States stood ready to remove any mines Iran tried to lay.)

The American Stake

Official U.S. policy toward the war did not waiver under the Carter and Reagan Administrations. The United States declared itself neutral; it supported the territorial integrity and political independence of both countries; it supported mediation efforts; and it said it would not sell weapons to either side. In fact, however, U.S. policy increasingly tilted toward Iraq.

The United States actually provided aid to both sides, while publicly leading a global campaign, Operation Staunch, to ban arms sales to Iran and force it to the negotiating table. The Reagan Administration sold arms secretly to the Tehran government in hopes of persuading Iran to order the release of American hostages held in Lebanon and to prevent the U.S.S.R. from gaining influence in Iran. Funds from the arms sales were used to support covertly the Nicaraguan counter-revolutionaries, or contras. When the arms-for-hostages deal was revealed in November 1986, the resulting scandal was widely viewed as a foreign policy disaster for the Reagan Administration.

The war's end was hastened when the United States and others concluded that it was too dangerous to be allowed to continue. Attacks on international shipping had increased in 1987, and Iran was sowing deadly mines in the Gulf and threatening to hit ships with Silkworm missiles. A strike by Iraqi aircraft on the U.S.S. *Stark* in May 1987 killed 37 American sailors. In order to persuade the Arab countries in the Gulf that the United States was not on Iran's side and to forestall Soviet inroads, the United States, at the request of Kuwait, sent an armada to the Gulf in July 1987. Its mission was to assure freedom of navigation and escort Kuwaiti oil tankers, which had been "reflagged," or transferred to U.S. registry.

The United States now turned to the UN in search of a solution. On July 20, 1987, the Security Council passed Resolution 598, which demanded a cease-fire, the withdrawal of forces to international boundaries, an exchange of prisoners, formal negotiations for a permanent settlement and the establishment of a tribunal to judge responsibility for the war. The resolution tilted in favor of Iraq, which promptly accepted it. Iran neither rejected nor accepted it.

In early 1988, Iraq stepped up military pressure on Iran. In March, Baghdad, the Iraqi capital, unleashed an estimated 150

Soviet-made missiles against Tehran, terrifying the population. It also used chemical weapons, which demoralized Iranian troops. A string of Iraqi victories on land, including the recapture of Fao, revealed Iran's weakness. The United States seized and blew up an Iranian vessel it caught red-handed laying mines in September 1987 and destroyed Iranian oil platforms in October 1987 and April 1988. Such actions helped persuade the Iranians that they could not win. The last straw was when the U.S.S. *Vincennes*, fearing it was about to be attacked by Iran, mistakenly downed an Iranian civilian airliner in July, killing 290 on board. To the surprise of all, Ayatollah Khomeini decided to "swallow poison," accept UN Resolution 598 and end the war. A cease-fire has been in effect since August 20, 1988.

Aftermath and Lessons

The Iran-Iraq war was the longest and one of the costliest conventional wars of this century. Casualties were estimated at over a million, with approximately 370,000 killed and 700,000 injured on both sides. When the war ended, neither side had achieved its aims and each felt that outside powers had cheated it out of victory. *The Economist* (London) commented, "This was a war that should never have been fought...neither side gained a thing, except the saving of its own regime. And neither regime was worth the sacrifice."

In both Iran and Iraq, but especially in the latter, the conflict and the demonization of the opponent led to a stronger sense of national identity. Iran's calculation that the Shiite majority in southern Iraq would rally to its cause and Iraq's conviction that the Arab citizens in Khuzistan would welcome the Iraqi army as their liberators were both wrong. The war helped the revolutionary government in Tehran consolidate power and distracted attention from pressing economic and social problems. Indeed, it was only when the leadership feared the revolution was in danger that it agreed to the cease-fire proposal.

The main reason for Western involvement in the war was to protect oil exports. Paradoxically, although there were short-term fluctuations, the price of oil did not go up but remained depressed, despite the war on shipping in the Persian Gulf.

The Iran-Iraq war was an anomaly for the Middle East because it was the first time the superpowers were on the same side. This partly resulted from Soviet preoccupation with its internal problems. Although both the United States and the Soviet Union professed neutrality, both in fact aided Iraq—the Soviet Union with arms, and the United States with economic, diplomatic and intelligence support—despite the fact that Iran was acknowledged to be the greater prize strategically. The superpowers' cooperation paved the way for greater unity during the Gulf war. The Iran-Iraq war also demonstrated the importance of the UN in conflict resolution.

The Persian Gulf War

Iraq's invasion of Kuwait on August 2, 1990, altered political alignments in the Middle East, imperiled world energy supplies and confronted the United States and the U.S.S.R. with the first international crisis since the end of the cold war. It also marked the resumption of Saddam Hussein's quest to dominate the Gulf.

The Iraqi leader evidently regarded the capture of Kuwait as a low-risk adventure that its Arab neighbors would be powerless to reverse. Iraq's active armed forces totaled one million, by far the largest in the region (Kuwait had an army of 20,000). They were battle tested and well armed. President Saddam Hussein also calculated that neither his ally, the Soviet Union, nor the United States would intervene. The United States, critics argue, gave Saddam a "green light" to invade or at least passed up an opportunity to warn him off.

"The mistake in the Arab world as well as the West was not to recognize the desperation of Saddam's situation," according to Middle East scholars Lawrence Freedman and Efraim Karsh. Iraq was in dire financial straits. Whereas Iran at the end of the war had virtually no foreign debt, Iraq was left owing as much as $80 billion, about half to Saudi Arabia, Kuwait and the UAE. Although the Saudis did not press for reimbursement, Kuwait showed no readiness to forgive or reduce the debt. Kuwait and the UAE also deliberately flooded the oil market in violation of production quotas set by the Organization of Petroleum Exporting Countries (OPEC), which depressed the price and hurt Iraq. In addition, Iraq charged that Kuwait was unfairly drawing oil from the giant Rumaila field which straddled their common border. In February and July 1990, President Saddam Hussein demanded more money from the Gulf states but they turned him down.

Saddam Hussein also needed to keep his huge army occupied. In a way, Kuwait would be a consolation prize for his failure to wrest Khuzistan from Iran. Gaining Kuwait would solve Iraq's financial problems and give Iraq a fine harbor on the Gulf. It would also lessen tension with Iran since it would greatly reduce the significance of who controlled the Shatt al-Arab.

The Western powers responded promptly to the invasion of Kuwait. President George Bush declared that "the acquisition of territory by force is unacceptable" and demanded Iraq's "unconditional and complete withdrawal." In announcing the dispatch of U.S. forces to Saudi Arabia in Operation Desert Shield on August 8, Bush declared that "a line has been drawn in the sand" to forestall an Iraqi invasion of Saudi Arabia. Economic sanctions and a naval embargo were placed on Iraq, and during the fall Americans—and others—debated whether these moves would have any effect.

By its forceful response to the crisis, the United States demonstrated that the "Vietnam syndrome"—the aversion to foreign involvement that gripped Americans in the wake of the Vietnam War (1963–75)—was over. In explaining his decision to send troops, President Bush said that the independence of Saudi Arabia was "of vital interest" to the United States. He insisted that if President Saddam Hussein got away with annexing Kuwait, world order would be endangered.

There was widespread confusion, however, over U.S. objectives. In November Bush declared, "The fight isn't about oil. The fight is about naked aggression that will not stand." Bush compared Saddam to the German führer Adolf Hitler and emphasized the dangers of appeasement. But later Secretary of State James A. Baker III, pointing to the war's economic consequences, said the main reason the United States was in Saudi Arabia was to protect American jobs.

President Bush sought above all to make it clear that Iraq, by its act of aggression, stood condemned not by the United States alone but by the world. In this he was largely successful. He mobilized an international coalition against Iraq and initiated a series of resolutions in the UN Security Council, including one calling for an embargo on trade with Iraq and another which authorized the use of force against Iraq if it did not withdraw from Kuwait by January 15, 1991. By that time, there were 560,000 U.S. troops in the Gulf in preparation for a ground war.

One of the most striking aspects of the crisis was the unprecedented degree of superpower cooperation. In truth, at the time, the Soviet Union was not in a position to oppose the United States. The very survival of the Soviet state was in question as communism crumbled in Eastern Europe and the government in Moscow moved toward a more-open political system and market-oriented economy. It would need U.S. aid to carry out its reforms.

The Regional Response

The crisis in the Gulf took Middle Easterners by surprise, so much so that the Kuwaiti royalty barely had time to escape. By inviting American troops to defend the kingdom, the Al Saud risked condemnation by fellow Arabs (and Saudis themselves) for giving outside powers, and non-Muslims at that, a chance to gain a foothold in the region. Partly thanks to the persuasive powers of Egypt's President Hosni Mubarak, a majority of the Arab League, which represents 20 Arab nations and the Palestine Liberation Organization (PLO), approved a resolution sending Arab forces to join U.S., British and French troops in Saudi Arabia.

Although it did not take part in the Persian Gulf war, Iran was a beneficiary. At the outset of the war, Saddam Hussein, in order to neutralize Iran, accepted the Iranian position on sharing the Shatt al-Arab waterway. Iran condemned the presence of U.S. forces in the Gulf, but it also called for the restoration of the ruling family in Kuwait. By not opposing the alliance against Iraq, Iran earned a measure of the West's gratitude and had the satisfaction of seeing its former enemy's military potential severely curtailed. It is especially significant that Iran refrained from giving much assistance to the postwar Shiite revolt in southern Iraq.

The 'Mother of all Battles'

After a tortured national debate that lasted throughout the fall of 1990, Congress voted on January 12, 1991, to authorize the use of force to remove the Iraqi army from Kuwait if it did not comply with a UN Security Council resolution and withdraw within three days. Saddam Hussein ignored the deadline, and allied air strikes began on January 16. Iraq's response was indecisive, with no major attack on the allied forces and only SCUD missile attacks on Saudi Arabia, Bahrain and Israel. Following more than a month of bombing, which pulverized Iraq's infrastructure, an allied ground assault, "Desert Storm," began on February 23. In 100 hours, allied forces recaptured Kuwait. Before retreating, the Iraqis set fire to 800 Kuwaiti oil wells, which burned for several months, and discharged 6 million to 8 million gallons of oil into the Gulf.

The question of why the United States abruptly halted Desert Storm and did not pursue Saddam Hussein's forces has haunted those who fought the war. At the time, the Administration was concerned that if it marched on Baghdad and overthrew the government, it would lose the support of its Arab allies and find itself in a quagmire. It was not willing to assume responsibility for administering Iraq and had no UN mandate to do so. The United States also did not want to weaken Iraq to such an extent that it could no longer check the power of Iran. In retrospect, many believe that the United States stopped the war too soon. At the very moment that Gen. Norman Schwarzkopf, the allied commander, was announcing in Riyadh, capital of Saudi Arabia, that "the gate is closed" and

Iraqi troops were trapped, two thirds of Iraq's elite Republican Guard were escaping. Continuing the war for another day or two could have assured the guard's destruction.

American casualties were miraculously few: only 148 Americans were killed in action (including 35 by "friendly fire"), and 467 were wounded. However, in the years following the war, some 100,000 veterans of the 700,000 who served in the Gulf asked for special medical screenings because of ailments they attribute to chemicals present in the battle zone. In August 1996, the Pentagon admitted for the first time that it did possess evidence that chemical weapons had been employed in the area. It is possible that up to 100,000 troops may have been exposed to nerve gas released when they blew up a massive Iraqi ammunition depot at Kamisiyah, Iraq, in March 1991.

For the Iraqi people, the results of the war were devastating. Initial estimates of 100,000 soldiers killed and 300,000 wounded, however, were wildly inflated. The Pentagon has not released an official estimate, but the House Armed Services Committee has put the number at 9,000 dead and 17,000 wounded. A former military analyst with the Defense Intelligence Agency estimates that there were some 1,500 Iraqi soldiers killed and 3,000 wounded, and fewer than 1,000 civilian deaths.

There is no doubt about the physical destruction of Iraq. A UN team that visited in March 1991 found that the bombardment had "wrought near apocalyptic results upon the infrastructure.... Iraq has...been relegated to a preindustrial age, but with all the...postindustrial dependency on an intensive use of energy and technology." By 1996, with water and sewage systems still in ruins, food production had fallen 30 percent, and 4,500 children were dying each month because of hunger or disease, according to the UN Children's Fund (Unicef). Before sanctions were imposed, Iraq had imported $360 million worth of drugs a year; in 1996 the figures dropped to about $33 million. Iraq reportedly has experienced a serious brain drain due to the emigration of its foreign-educated elite.

Despite the allied triumph on the battlefield and the restoration of the Kuwaiti government, critics claimed the United States had won the war but lost the peace. Saddam Hussein remained in power and lost no time in crushing rebellions by Shiite Arabs in the south and Kurds in the north—rebellions that the United States had encouraged. President Bush later acknowledged that mistakes had been made in the armistice meeting at Safwan, Iraq, after the war. At that time, General Schwarzkopf gave Iraq permission to fly armed helicopters anywhere inside the country, as long as they stayed away from American forces. This enabled Saddam Hussein to crush the uprisings.

Unfinished Business

At the end of the Persian Gulf war, the allied coalition imposed stringent conditions on Iraq which, more than seven years after the conflict, seriously restrict its sovereignty. Under UN Resolution 687 of April 1991, Iraq is required to disclose the extent of its programs to develop chemical, nuclear and biological weapons and ballistic missiles and to dismantle them. Iraq also had to agree to long-term UN monitoring. Only after the UN had confirmed that Iraq was not rearming could sanctions be lifted. For years Baghdad has engaged in a cat-and-mouse game with UN inspectors, who have installed a monitoring system but are not yet satisfied that Iraq is in full compliance. According to Bill Richardson, U.S. ambassador to the UN, "Getting Iraq to comply is like pulling teeth from somebody who doesn't want to open up his mouth."

Most worrisome is Iraq's nuclear program. Iraq reportedly had pursued a crash program to build a bomb by April 1991, which the allied attack interrupted. Whether it could have met the deadline is debatable. Iraq's chemical- and biological-weapons programs are also a continuing concern. In November 1997, Iraq's temporary refusal to allow Americans to participate in the inspections led to a crisis that was resolved by Russian diplomacy.

Under a UN resolution that took effect in December 1996 and was renewed in June and December 1997, Iraq is allowed

The Kurds: 'No Friends but the Mountains'

ALTHOUGH THE WAR against Iraq resulted in a great victory for the allied forces, it led to tragedy for the Kurds. An ancient Middle Eastern nation numbering an estimated 30 million, the Kurds are dispersed among Turkey (where they constitute around 24 percent of the country's population), Iraq (21 percent), Iran (11 percent), Syria (10 percent) and the former Soviet Union. They comprise the largest ethnic group in the Middle East after the Arabs, Persians and Turks, and are one of the largest nations today with no state of their own. The majority are Sunni Muslims and speak Kurdish, an Iranian language. About half of all Kurds live in cities. Traditionally, Kurds have given their allegiance to extended families and clans, not purely political figures.

After World War I, the Kurds were one of the minorities who did not gain their own independent state. The fragmented Kurdish community has struggled for greater autonomy within the various countries ever since. Iranian Kurds briefly established their own Soviet-backed republic in 1945–46. Only in Iraq, however, have they posed a continuing threat to the rule of the central government. Turkey has attempted to suppress the Kurds living within its borders (it refers to them as "mountain Turks"), which has prompted Western charges of human-rights abuse. Since 1987, the Turkish government has been locked in a bitter conflict with the main opposition group, the Kurdish Workers party (PKK).

During Iraq's war with Iran in the 1980s, Kurdish rebels took control of large parts of northern Iraq. However, after the cease-fire in August 1988, Iraqi forces struck back with a vengeance. They destroyed Kurdish villages and transferred their populations to detention camps in other parts of the country. Most heinous, however, was the Iraqis' use of chemical weapons. In March 1988 Iraq gassed an estimated 4,000 civilians in the border city of Halabjah.

In March 1991, after allied forces had routed the Iraqi army, a popular uprising broke out among Shiites of southern Iraq. It was quickly followed by Kurdish insurrection in which Kurdish rebels seized much of northern Iraq. The United States did not want to see the emergence of an independent Kurdistan and did not aid the rebels. Forces loyal to Saddam Hussein brutally turned on the Kurds, causing at least 1.5 million refugees to flee to the Turkish and Iranian border areas. The United States, Britain and France, with the cooperation of Turkey, then instituted a relief effort and pledged that the Kurdish zone would remain a safe haven. Primary elections were held for a regional government in 1992, as Iraqi Kurdistan became in effect independent. However, Iraq imposed a blockade and kept the Kurdish zone partially cut off from the rest of the country, as its economy, like that of the rest of Iraq, deteriorated.

The two principal Iraqi Kurdish groups are the Kurdistan Democratic party (KDP), led by Massoud Barzani, and the Patriotic Union of Kurdistan (PUK), led by Jalal Talabani. Barzani and Talabani are traditional clan leaders who are bitter rivals. Each represents a different subdivision of Kurds (Barzani is from northern Kurdistan and Talabani from central Kurdistan), and each speaks a different dialect.

Outsiders have historically manipulated Kurdish political factions, which has hindered Kurdish unity. The KDP's request in 1996 for Iraqi assistance to retake the city of Arbil, Iraq, from the PUK (backed by Iran) struck many Kurds as a betrayal that allowed the Baghdad government to begin to reestablish its authority in the north. The United States mediated a cease-fire between the two factions in October 1996, but this broke down when fighting started again in October 1997. One scenario that neighboring countries, as well as external powers, do not want to see is the emergence of an independent Kurdistan. As the Kurds like to say, when the chips are down, they have no friends but the mountains.

to sell $2 billion worth of oil every six months, with the UN closely supervising the disbursement of funds. Designed to alleviate civilian suffering, the resolution authorizes Iraq to use the proceeds to buy food and medicines, pay for war reparations and reimburse the UN monitoring operation. This was the first significant infusion of funds Iraq had received in six years.

The Border Issue

Under the terms of the UN cease-fire resolution, a commission was formed to determine the *de jure* border between Iraq and Kuwait. It did so in April 1992. The new official border benefits Kuwait by granting it a large part of the Rumaila oil field and the southern part of Iraq's port of Umm Qasr. The main navigation lanes of Khawr Abdullah inlet, which are located to the north of the islands of Bubiyan and Warba and provide access to Umm Qasr, have now been defined to lie in Kuwaiti waters.

These boundary revisions angered Iraq, although it formally accepted them in November 1994. "Territorial stability will probably come to this part of the world only when Iraq reconciles itself to its disadvantageous position at the head of the Gulf, when it perceives itself as no longer 'squeezed out,'" according to geographer Richard Schofield. In his opinion, "the integrated, or at least coordinated, economic development of the northern Gulf seems to offer the best hope of future stability and the only probable means by which future Iraqi governments would ultimately come to terms with their restricted access to Gulf waters."

The Internal Revolts

Following Baghdad's brutal suppression of the internal revolts by Shiites in the south and Kurds in the north after the war, the UN Security Council adopted Resolution 688, which demanded that the Iraqi government stop suppressing its own citizens, especially in the Kurdish areas. The allied powers and neighboring states agreed that they would not recognize an independent Kurdish state, but the United States, in cooperation with Turkey, Britain and France, started operation "Provide Comfort." To assure a safe haven for the Kurds, Iraqi forces were forbidden from flying fixed-wing aircraft above the 36th parallel. After the French withdrawal from air patrols in 1997, the operation was renamed Northern Watch.

Ever since the war, Iraqi Kurdistan, with a population of some 3.5 million, has been in a state of political limbo. (See pages 38–39.) The two main Kurdish political groups, the Kurdistan Democratic party (KDP) and the Patriotic Union of Kurdistan (PUK), have not been able to cooperate in administering the region. The governments in Baghdad and Tehran have taken advantage of the disorder to intervene militarily there in support of their Kurdish allies, the KDP and PUK, respectively. The Turkish government has carried out cross-border attacks on Turkish Kurds (led by the Kurdish Workers party, or PKK) who are waging a guerrilla war against it and have sought refuge on the Iraqi side of the border. The persistent outside intervention led to U.S. warnings in October 1997 that Iran and Iraq must respect the no-fly zone, although no similar warning was issued to Turkey.

Since August 1992, the United States and its allies in the Gulf war, in order to provide a safe haven for the Shiites, have banned flights by Iraqi aircraft south of the 32nd parallel; in September 1996, this was extended to the 33rd parallel. This protection was originally provided after the United States realized that the Shiites, who opposed Saddam Hussein, were not about to ally with Iran but might help bring about Saddam's downfall. The objective was also to prevent Iraqi forces from massing for an attack on Kuwait or Saudi Arabia. Air cover, however, has not prevented Saddam Hussein from moving tanks and artillery into the region and decimating any opposition. The president has adopted a simpler expedient to crush the Marsh Arabs, or Madan. They are being punished for sympathizing with and aiding Shiite rebels. He is draining the marshes where they live, denying them refuge and in the process destroying their unique culture.

3

The Future of the Gulf:
Conflict or Cooperation?

THE SECOND PERSIAN Gulf war, by placing the states and their rulers in a media spotlight, helped to open up closed societies and to raise expectations among their people for future change. Commented dissident Iraqi writer Kanan Makiya: "The Iraqi pillage of Kuwait has lifted the lid on the historic failure of Arab political culture to deal with questions of democracy, citizenship, ethnic minorities and, above all, the right of individuals, communities and states to be separate and different."

The challenges facing the Gulf states may be divided into external ones, notably security threats from neighboring countries, the arms race and border tensions, and internal problems, including weak economies and rising unemployment, the threat of political Islam and demands for greater political participation. All hold the potential for conflict or cooperation.

The Arms Race

In an address to Congress in March 1991 after the victory in Desert Storm, President Bush declared, "It would be tragic if the nations of the Middle East and Persian Gulf were now, in the wake of war, to embark on a new arms race." He advocated controlling the proliferation of nuclear weapons and missiles, but did not mention the reduction of conventional arms sales. In the aftermath of war, GCC defense expenditures rose, partly driven by a perceived threat from Iran and Iraq. The Middle East continues to be the largest arms market in the world, and the United States the main supplier. In 1996, the value of worldwide arms sales was $31.8 billion; sales to developing countries were $19.4 billion. Saudi Arabia is by far the largest arms buyer in the developing world. For the period 1993–96, arms transfer agreements with the GCC states from all suppliers were as follows: Saudi Arabia ($20.3 billion); Kuwait ($5.3 billion); UAE ($5.2 billion); Qatar ($2.2 billion); Oman ($700 million); and Bahrain ($300 million). In 1996, Saudi Arabia's defense budget stood at $17 billion, Iran's $3.3 billion, Kuwait's $3.5 billion and the UAE's $2 billion.

The military balance between Iran and Iraq was at rough parity in late 1996, but over the next five years Iran will develop a significant advantage as it expands its ground forces, according to Dr. Andrew Rathmell, a security analyst at King's College, London. "Tehran often argues that its arms purchases are merely a response to the weak position it found itself in at the end of war with Iraq. While it is true that Iran's inventory of hardware was badly depleted, its current acquisition programs are set to turn it into the regional superpower over the next decade." In rearming, Iran has given priority to its maritime capabilities. It has bought three small submarines from Russia and antiship cruise missiles from China. It is attempting to acquire medium- and long-range ballistic missiles from China and North Korea, and it has increased its capability to manufacture its own arms. In September 1997, the U.S. and Israeli governments expressed alarm that Iran, with aid from Russia and China, was rapidly developing a ballistic-missile program that could threaten neighboring states within the next few years.

The most serious threats to Gulf security are Iran and Iraq's programs to develop weapons of mass destruction. At present, it is unclear whether Iraq's nuclear program is defunct, and the country is believed to have hidden some of its chemical and biological weapons. There is little question that Tehran has been surreptitiously laying the groundwork for building a nuclear weapon. How long this would take is a matter of speculation. In March 1997 the head of the U.S. Arms Control and Disarmament Agency said Iran was at least eight years away from producing a bomb. Iran denies it intends to produce such weapons. As a party to the 1968 Treaty on the Non-Proliferation of Nuclear Weapons (NPT), Iran is legally entitled to develop nuclear energy and in the future hopes to obtain 20 percent of its energy from this source. It permits the International Atomic Energy Agency (IAEA) to inspect its nuclear research facilities, and so far its inspectors have not found any activities inconsistent with peaceful uses. In 1995, Russia agreed to complete a nuclear power plant, begun by Germany in the late 1970s, at Bushire on the Gulf coast. Over U.S. objections, Russia contracted to provide a 1,000-megawatt nuclear reactor for the plant, to be completed in the year 2000, and may provide a second unit there in the future. The United States strongly opposes these deals for fear that Iran will use the expertise it gains to develop a nuclear weapon. (China signed a contract in 1993 to build two nuclear power plants on the Karun River south of Ahwaz and two more near Bushire, but the fate of these plants is unclear due to heavy U.S. pressure on China to cancel the deals.)

Border Tensions

When Iraq invaded Kuwait in August 1990, the Baghdad government claimed it was merely regaining by force what rightfully belonged to it, since historically Kuwait was an "integral part of Iraq." Such recourse to the past, often to colonial arrangements decided during or after World War I, is common in the Gulf. Several of the most intractable disputes that have the potential to escalate into armed clashes have roots in the colonial period. These include differences between Iraq and Kuwait over land and marine boundaries; between Iran and the UAE over Abu Musa and the Tunbs; between Iran and Iraq over the Shatt al-Arab waterway; and between Qatar and Bahrain over the Hawar Islands.

Many of the more "solvable" disputes have been settled in recent years. Finalizing the area's political map, according to geographer Schofield, was necessary to facilitate oil exploration and development. Even when "solved," however, old border disputes tend to break out anew when tension between states arises. For example, in their 1971 memorandum of understanding, Iran and Sharja agreed to share the administration of the island of Abu Musa without surrendering either's claim to sovereignty. This arrangement worked well for two decades, but when relations between Iran and the UAE deteriorated, the validity of the understanding was called into question. Schofield notes that Iraq's border disputes with Iran and Kuwait follow an alternating pattern: when relations with Iran are strained over the Shatt al-Arab, Iraq increases demands on Kuwait for access to the islands.

The Future of Iraq

The greatest question in the region is how long Saddam Hussein will stay in power. He has survived numerous coup attempts as well as major internal revolts, but he still exercises iron control over the country. There is no organized resistance inside Iraq, and the opposition in exile is badly fragmented. Some members of the Sunni community regard Saddam Hussein as a protector.

The type of leader and government that replaces Saddam Hussein will be crucial to regional stability. Many outside Iraq, including opposition groups, hope and assume that a new government will reverse previous policies. However, this is not necessarily so, cautions Charles Tripp, senior lecturer in politics at the University of London. The most likely candidates to carry out a coup, he points out, are Sunni Arab army officers who supported the president's attacks on Iran and Kuwait and ruthlessly put down uprisings by the Shiites and Kurds. They want the military to maintain its privileged position in Iraqi society and a government that continues to rule Iraq as it has been ruled for decades—through a small "community of trust" made up of kinsmen who will not betray each other. Such men share a sense of humiliation imposed by outsiders and would probably continue to feel suspicious of the intentions of neighboring countries. In short, a future Iraqi government is likely to bear a considerable resemblance to past ones.

End of the Holiday

Although outsiders generally imagine the Gulf monarchies to be fabulously wealthy, this is no longer the case. As *The Financial Times* (London) put it, "Saudi Arabia was briefly a rich country." Although the Gulf states enjoyed a huge financial windfall for about two decades, the price of oil collapsed in 1986; the average price of crude oil fell to $14 per barrel from over $34 in 1981. Their economies are highly dependent upon oil income. Saudi Arabia, for example, relies on oil for three quarters of its revenues. Iran and Iraq have experienced a drastic drop in production in recent years and suffer most from a decline in the price of oil. Before its revolution, Iran was producing 6 million barrels of oil a day; its current production is around 3.7 million. Iraq exported virtually no oil for over six years, which has cost the country $100 billion in revenues and led to the pauperization of its citizens.

As oil revenues weakened, populations have grown, leading to a significant drop in per capita income. And because of the 2.4 percent rate of population growth in the six Gulf monarchies—way above the world average of 1.5 percent—unemployment is a growing problem, especially in Bahrain, Oman and Saudi Arabia. Over one third of the people in the Gulf monarchies, Iraq and Iran today are under the age of 15. The population is not only young but highly urbanized: about 85 percent of the residents of the GCC states now live in cities.

They are not receiving the education and training needed to enter the labor market.

The composition of the labor force is also problematic. Due to the shortage of workers with technical skills for high-end jobs and a widespread unwillingness to perform manual labor for low-end ones, the Gulf governments depend to a large extent on expatriate labor. Foreign workers now account for 90 percent of the labor force in the UAE, 83 percent in Qatar, 82 percent in Kuwait, 69 percent in Saudi Arabia and around 60 percent in Bahrain and Oman. By the year 2010, another 8 million people are expected to enter the labor market, yet there will not be enough jobs for them. Warns Kuwaiti economist Jassem al-Saadoun, "Planners and decisionmakers must... attempt to create enough jobs for the newcomers or face the alternative—severe unemployment, with possibilities of social and political extremism. All available signs point to the latter happening."

Governments are under pressure to introduce structural economic reforms such as reducing their subsidies and burgeoning bureaucracies, privatization and imposing more taxes, but inertia has prevented them from attracting more outside investment, especially in the oil industry. Potential foreign investors are hindered by a lack of business information, monopolies and lack of government support. The most lucrative sectors of the economy, including oil and franchises for foreign products, continue to be off-limits to outsiders. A sensitive issue is that of the royal families and the favoritism enjoyed by their members. In Saudi Arabia, for example, there are thousands of princes on the state payroll, and it is difficult to remove them. An often-mentioned remedy to reduce the bloated public sector is to privatize government-owned companies. Kuwait and Oman have made some progress in this direction. Privatization, however, is not a cure as long as there is no real competition. Moreover, it will likely accelerate the problem of unemployment and consequently lead to political unrest.

The political implications of stagnating economies and growing populations in the Gulf monarchies are now becoming apparent. Governments can no longer afford to provide an array of benefits, including guaranteed employment for college graduates. In Kuwait, where 92 percent of those working in 1996 were employed by the government, the country spends half of its oil income on salaries. The rentier state, while still in existence, is breaking down or changing. The high cost of the Persian Gulf war (Saudi Arabia alone contributed $55 billion) dissipated the financial cushion these countries had built up. Today people throughout the Gulf are questioning government decisions and demanding more accountability. There is little evidence to date, though, that Gulf monarchies are serious about making reforms. The ruling families are reluctant to give up their traditional prerogatives, and they believe that oil prices will soon rise and rescue their foundering economies. (However, while demand remains strong, the world oil market faces a supply glut in 1998, according to the International Energy Agency. By late 1997 the price of oil had gone back down to around $18 a barrel, after a brief rise in 1996, due to the continued growth of non-OPEC supplies, OPEC's inability to enforce its quotas and the availability of some Iraqi crude.) The outlook for the economies of the Gulf states over the coming years depends very much on the price of oil, which is uncertain.

The Case of Iran

Iran today is an authoritarian state. Yet members of parliament engage in genuine debate, and publications representing a wide variety of political viewpoints are available. There is particularly intense questioning of the role of the ulama (Muslim religious scholars) in governance and whether it would be better for them and for Islam if they were to return to the mosques and advise the government rather than run it. This is a position advocated by a popular Iranian philosopher with impeccable Islamic credentials, Dr. Abdolkarim Soroush, whom the regime has tried to silence. Soroush believes that Islam and democracy are compatible and that medieval Islamic texts can be reinterpreted in light of modern conditions. In late 1997,

Reuters/Str/Archive Photos

Mohammad Khatami, elected president of Iran in a surprising
landslide vote on May 23, 1997, waves to supporters as he
leaves a polling station.

the role of the country's spiritual leader, Ayatollah Ali
Khamenei, was openly questioned by dissident clerics, as pressures grew to liberalize the political system. Growing calls to
limit his extensive powers were bitterly resisted by conserva-
tives.

By all accounts the generation that has grown up with the
revolution—about half the population—has resisted religious
indoctrination and is very cynical about clerical rule. This was
reflected in the election of Mohammad Khatami, 54, as president. His defeat of the expected winner, hard-liner Ali Akbar
Nateq-Nuri, was aided in large measure by young people and
women and was regarded as a repudiation of existing policies.
While one of the clerical elite, Khatami is known for modera-
tion, tolerance, respect for the rule of law and promising to restore personal freedoms. Nateq-Nuri, however, remains the
speaker of parliament and is in a position to block new policies.

Ali Akbar Hashemi-Rafsanjani (president from 1989 to 1997) is still politically active as head of the Expediency Council, the country's highest legislative body. Many Iranians who have felt betrayed by the revolution now have reason to hope for a better future. In December 1997, Iran's surprise qualification for the World Cup soccer finals led to unprecedented scenes of mass public celebration and dancing in the streets that the government could not stop.

The Iranian Economy

The economic situation in Iran is much worse than in the Gulf monarchies. The reason for this is simple: income from oil exports is only one third of what it was at the time of the revolution, whereas the population has almost doubled. Domestic oil and gas consumption has more than doubled since the revolution, and if it continues to rise, Iran could cease to be a major exporter of energy. Part of the problem is that gasoline is very cheap due to government subsidies; even after a price hike in April 1997, regular gas only costs twenty cents a gallon.

The greatest complaint among Iranians today is the poor standard of living. The minimum wage is $2.80 a day, and even university professors may make only a little over $100 a month. In order for Iran's economy to improve, a number of things are needed, including higher oil and gas prices, a unified exchange rate, less state regulation, less corruption and greater privatization. Government-controlled foundations, or *bonyads*, currently dominate much of the economy and are universally regarded as inefficient and corrupt. Many professionals fled abroad with the revolution, and the authorities have not yet provided the guarantees needed to entice them back. So far, it is unclear when and if serious structural problems will be addressed.

Iran's economy, nevertheless, is now stronger than it has been in five years. Inflation, estimated at 50 percent for 1996, was expected to drop in 1997. A steep reduction in imports over the past few years has allowed Iran to make headway in paying off its foreign debt, which rose to over $30 billion in the early 1990s. Iran possesses the second-largest reserves of natural gas in the world after Russia, and, while it does not currently export it in commercial quantities, expects to do so in the next few years. However, U.S. trade sanctions have hindered the huge investment that is required. Iran also faces competition from Qatar.

Although Arab Gulf states remain wary of Iranian intentions in the Gulf, they regarded the election of President Khatami as a positive sign and an opportunity to improve relations. Iran has indicated that better ties with the Gulf Arabs is a top foreign policy goal. It has repeatedly expressed interest in confidence-building measures in the Gulf, that is, measures to make military activities more predictable and transparent, leading to mutual trust between hostile states. In the fall of 1997, Iran-Saudi ties warmed with the resumption of commercial air links, Iran and Bahrain normalized diplomatic relations 15 months after they had been broken off, and foreign ministers of the GCC states called for a new relationship with Iran based on trust.

The major obstacle to better Arab-Iranian relations is the dispute over the islands, with neither Iran nor the UAE yet ready to retreat from claims of full sovereignty over Abu Musa and the Tunbs. In addition, Iran's main goal—the removal of outside forces from the Gulf and the assumption by littoral states of Gulf security—implies that Iran would dominate the Gulf. At present it is highly unlikely that the GCC states would willingly relinquish American protection.

Toward a Civil Society?

Whether the Persian Gulf states are an exception to the worldwide trend toward greater democratization is an issue much debated by scholars of the region. It is true that the Gulf countries have no political parties, trade unions or free press. Government traditionally has bought off or suppressed potential opposition. The "private sector" in the Gulf is based on kinship relations and works closely with the government to maintain a favored position. It may have neither the power nor the inclination to force major changes in nondemocratic political regimes.

Other observers believe changes are now under way. Civil groups—professional associations, chambers of commerce, human-rights advocates and Islamist groups—are being formed and are pressing governments to make reforms. They are pushing in each state, in varying degrees, for greater input in the decisionmaking process.

In the wake of the Gulf war, political, professional and religious groups in a number of countries, including Kuwait, Saudi Arabia, Bahrain and Qatar, petitioned their governments for greater freedoms, increased means of political participation, stricter adherence to Islamic law and more accountability on the part of the rulers. These petitions at the same time expressed support for ruling families and demanded reform, not revolution. In Saudi Arabia, Oman and Bahrain, governments have formed consultative councils, but the latter are appointed by the ruler who may or may not heed their advice. In Saudi Arabia, the king announced major reforms in 1992, including what amounted to the first-ever constitution. Oman followed suit in November 1996. Among the GCC countries, Kuwait allows the greatest degree of political freedom. Parliamentary life resumed after the Gulf war and elections were last held in 1996.

Information Technology

New technologies are playing an important role in opening up the Gulf to the outside world, and the information revolution has undermined rulers' monopoly of power. In both Iran and Saudi Arabia, satellite receivers, though banned, are in widespread use and bring CNN and MTV into many living rooms. The fax machine has made communication with the Gulf countries faster and more reliable and the government cannot censor what comes in.

The greatest agent for change may be the Internet. All of the Gulf states are on-line, with the exception of Iraq. (To mark the Iraqi president's 60th birthday in May 1997, a Baghdad computer firm set up a home page for Saddam Hussein—with an electronic mailbox in Jordan.) The heaviest Internet user in the region is Iran, with 30,000 subscribers. (The two leading candidates in the recent presidential election both established web sites in Persian.) In the UAE, there were over 10,000 subscribers in early 1997.

Governments long used to controlling the flow of information are uncomfortable that their citizens now can easily connect with the outside world. However, they recognize it is inevitable and even necessary for businesses to compete. But they monitor the Internet so that nothing "un-Islamic" is transmitted, meaning pornography and religious or political materials. Despite these restrictions, "Internet fever" is reported to be sweeping the Gulf.

The Role of Women

In Iran, the proper role for women is a hotly contested issue. Women played a major role in the Iranian revolution, and since then have been more vocal about obtaining equal rights. The goal of some revolutionaries was to purge the moral corruption that supposedly prevailed under the shah and this meant that women should not be "too Western" in appearance, wear makeup or socialize with men. The ruling Shiite clerics have restricted job opportunities for women and forced them to wear *hijab*, or what they define as "Islamicly correct," or modest, clothing. Since the election of President Khatami, women have increasingly tried to challenge the strict dress code.

In the Arabian peninsula, the role of women is more circumscribed than in Iran. Rulers who claim tribal and Islamic justification for their rule are loath to permit any changes in the private sphere of family life. Women are not allowed to vote, even in Kuwait, although in October 1997 a few women were allowed to stand for election to Oman's Consultative Council; two won.

The famous "driving incident" that took place in Saudi Arabia on November 6, 1990, illustrates just how sensitive public opinion is to any change in the status quo. At that time some 45 Saudi women met in a supermarket parking lot in Riyadh, dismissed their drivers, and publicly drove around, thus breaking an unwritten rule against women drivers. The government, prodded by objections from religious authorities, treated this as a serious challenge to its authority. It had the women fired from their jobs (most were teachers and university professors) and confiscated their passports. The ban against women driving was made official. Although the penalties were later quietly removed, the ban served as a warning to elite women seeking greater rights.

The Islamic Challenge in Saudi Arabia

The resurgence of religion in political life that has marked the Middle East since the 1970s for a long time seemed hardly to have touched Saudi Arabia, the most Islamic of states, which is ruled strictly according to the *Sharia*, or Islamic law. The second Gulf war changed everything. A bitter split has developed between the "official" religious establishment supported by the government and the outlawed opposition, which accuses the ruling Al Saud family of squandering national resources, being puppets of the West and not being sufficiently Islamic in their rule. They also criticized the *fatwa*, or ruling, issued by a senior religious scholar, allowing U.S. troops to enter Saudi Arabia. The Islamic opposition in Saudi Arabia is made up of young, middle-class and nontribal urbanites, and it is led by preachers from the government-funded religious universities. They complain about declining living standards and object in particular to Western cultural influence; hence the vehement protests at the time of the women's driving incident. "The postwar resurgence of Islamism was a reaffirmation of identity, a protest movement against the monarchy and its Western allies, and for some, a means to achieve social influence and, perhaps, a takeover of power," notes political scientist R. Hrair Dekmejian.

In February 1991 and September 1992, ulama predominantly from Najd presented unprecedented petitions to the Saudi government demanding reforms that would seriously curtail the power of the ruling family. In May 1993, six Islamists, led by physics professor Muhammad al-Masari, founded the Committee for the Defense of Legitimate Rights (CDLR).

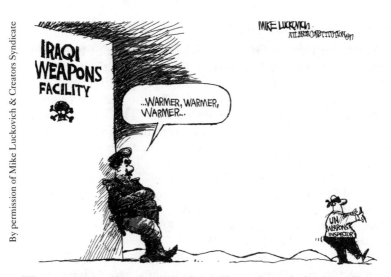

By permission of Mike Luckovich & Creators Syndicate

(The name in English is misleading, since it is actually concerned with Sharia rights, not human rights as generally understood.) The authorities quickly closed down the committee and Dr. Masari fled to Britain, where he has carried on his fight. The committee's main technique is to send hundreds of faxes each week back to Saudi Arabia accusing the royal family of corruption and demanding its overthrow. The CDLR claims it does not have political goals, but favors the imposition of Islamic law and calls for reform rather than revolution. It has sought to present itself to the Western media as moderate in its program, which remains rather unclear.

How much support does the Islamic opposition have in Saudi Arabia? At present it is more an annoyance to the ruling family than a real threat. The appeal of the CDLR's strict Wahhabi interpretation of Islam is not universal, having little attraction in the more liberal Hijaz region or among Saudi Shiites, who have their own opposition group. Nor does it appeal to the modern middle class. The Islamic opposition took an ominous turn with the bombings in Saudi Arabia of an American military training mission in Riyadh in November 1995 and U.S. military housing in Dhahran in June 1996.

The Uprising in Bahrain

Since the Persian Gulf war, the government of Bahrain has come under unprecedented pressure to restore the parliament, which was dissolved in 1975. The ruling amir did form a consultative council in December 1992, but the members are appointed and serve at his sufferance. The opposition has presented several petitions to the ruler, including one in October 1994 demanding a return to democracy, an end to corruption, a reduction in unemployment and a limitation on foreign labor. This was signed by 23,000 people, a majority of them (70 percent) Shiites and about one fifth women. Further petitions followed in 1995, including one signed by 310 women. Antigovernment uprisings broke out in December 1994 and have continued sporadically since then.

The government attempted to portray the opposition as simply a sectarian movement, disregarding the varied background (both Sunni and Shiite) of the petition signers. As violent incidents have grown, the government has targeted Shiite areas for retribution and the revolt has taken on more of a sectarian character. In what many interpreted as an attempt to shift blame and gain outside sympathy, in June 1996 the government publicly accused Iran of instigating the revolt. Most outside observers agree that the roots of the trouble are homegrown, and lie mainly in the high unemployment rate and corruption. Human Rights Watch attributes the current unrest largely to widespread violations of civil and political rights by the government and security forces. The government has shown little interest in reform or compromise and has brutally put down demonstrations. So far the Bahraini government has received the support of other GCC governments, especially that of Saudi Arabia. Because the problems the Gulf monarchies face are present in more extreme form in Bahrain, many wonder if this island-state is a bellwether of the region's future.

The Succession

Succession to power is a key issue in all the Gulf states. The only country in which the process has become predictable is

Iran, with its constitutional provisions for presidential election. In Iraq, Saddam Hussein may remain in power for some time, or he may be assassinated tomorrow. The likelihood is for a struggle when he departs. The Arab Gulf states are ruled for the most part by long-standing monarchs who in the coming years will begin passing from the scene. (The last change in leadership in Oman was in 1970; in Bahrain and the UAE, 1971; in Kuwait, 1977; and in Saudi Arabia, 1982.) Only in Qatar has a member of the younger generation come to the throne, in this case when Prince Hamad, then 45, overthrew his father in 1995. Hamad is proving to be a maverick in the region, promising more political liberalization and showing a readiness to maintain ties with Israel, Iraq and Iran. Like other Gulf royals of his generation, he is more Westernized than many of his countrymen.

In the key state of Saudi Arabia, King Fahd is ailing and likely will soon be succeeded by Crown Prince Abdullah, the commander of the National Guard, and Abdullah, in turn, by Defense Minister Prince Sultan. But these men are both over 70, and after them the succession could go to one of the next generation, the grandsons of Ibn Saud—which could involve a struggle. So far the Gulf monarchies have been fortunate in the successions that have taken place, but the future is uncertain as more princes will compete for power.

◆ტ

Despite the rapid economic development that has transformed the landscape of the Persian Gulf countries over the past few decades, they lag behind other regions in terms of political liberalization, while their economies have serious structural problems. The Gulf monarchs have staked their future on continued strong demand and higher prices for their oil, which is not at all certain. Iraq faces a major, prolonged task of rebuilding after UN sanctions are lifted. The potential economic crisis in Iran is particularly troubling. Without outside investment, Iran as well as Iraq will be prevented from modernizing its oil and gas export potential, which is the key to economic viability.

4

U.S. Policy:
Retrospect and Prospects

THE UNITED STATES IS A RELATIVE latecomer to the Middle
East. After World War II, it became the dominant external force in Iran and Saudi Arabia as the Soviets gained influence in Iraq. Britain remained the predominant influence in
the smaller Persian Gulf countries and the main naval power in
the Gulf. Until 1971, when Britain voluntarily withdrew, the
United States relied on it to guarantee political stability there.
Afterward, Washington counted on the "twin pillars" of Iran
and Saudi Arabia to keep the oil flowing and to oppose possible
Soviet inroads. The Iranian revolution and the fall of the shah
in January 1979 created a power vacuum in the Gulf.

The "loss" of Iran, combined with the Soviet intervention
in Afghanistan in December 1979, led the Carter Administration to regard the region as a "crescent of crisis." In a January
1980 address to Congress, the U.S. President warned the Soviet Union that "an attempt by any outside force to gain control

of the Persian Gulf region…will be repelled by the use of any means necessary, including military force."

When military force was introduced, however, it was used not against an external power but a regional one. In the 1980s it became clear that the major threat to stability did not come from the Soviet Union but from the military confrontation between Iran and Iraq. The main U.S. interest in the first Gulf war was to protect Saudi Arabia and the Arab Gulf states from an Iranian attack, and in the second Gulf war, from an Iraqi attack. President Bush declared that the independence of Saudi Arabia was "of vital interest" to the United States and drew "a line in the sand" to protect it.

If Iraqi President Saddam Hussein had seized Saudi Arabia, he would have had control over 40 percent of the world's oil supplies and a stranglehold on the world's economy. Oil, indeed, was a major reason for the unprecedented U.S. commitment. "Laid bare, American policy in the Gulf comes down to this: troops have been sent to retain control of oil in the hands of a pro-American Saudi Arabia so prices will remain low," wrote Thomas L. Friedman, then a diplomatic correspondent for *The New York Times*.

The United States is in a stronger position today in the Gulf than ever before, and it has fully assumed Britain's earlier security role. Arab monarchs who formerly wanted American forces kept "over the horizon" now acknowledge, however uncomfortably, their dependence. The U.S. strategy is largely a naval one, with Bahrain serving as the headquarters for the U.S. Fifth Fleet. Kuwait and Qatar have allowed the United States to preposition military supplies. In 1980, at the time the Carter Doctrine was announced, it would have taken the United States three months to send a military division to the Gulf. In 1990, this could be accomplished in three weeks, and in 1994, three days.

During the Desert Storm campaign, an international alliance achieved the common goal of ending Iraq's occupation of Kuwait. This was the way the new world order was supposed to work, with the United States and Soviet Union cooperating to achieve a common policy aim. The wartime coalition, however, has now broken up, and it is questionable whether—absent a clearcut case of aggression—another one could be organized. During the standoff with Saddam Hussein's government in November 1997, the former U.S. allies opposed taking any military action against Iraq. The crisis also marked the return of Russia as a player in regional diplomacy for the first time since Desert Storm.

Dual Containment

After the British departure, the United States sought to foster a balance of power in the Gulf by playing off the shah's Iran against Iraq, and later, after the Iranian revolution, Saddam Hussein's Iraq against the Islamic Republic of Iran. The idea of using one power to check the other has now been abandoned in favor of pressuring both. This policy, called dual containment, was introduced in May 1993, several months after President Clinton took office. Dual containment aims to maintain a strong U.S. presence in the region to deter Iran and Iraq from asserting hegemony over the Gulf or acquiring nuclear weapons. At the same time, it seeks to bolster the individual and collective defense capabilities of the GCC states. The United States has, in effect, three Gulf policies: one for the GCC states, one for Iran and one for Iraq. The failure to integrate the policies stems in part from a longtime reluctance inherited from Britain to view the Persian Gulf as a whole.

The Administration has tried to force both of these "outlaw states" to pay a high price for remaining outside the democratic family of nations. "As the sole superpower, the United States has a special responsibility for developing a strategy to neutralize, contain and, through selective pressure, perhaps eventually transform these backlash states into constructive members of the international community," according to Anthony Lake, former assistant to the President for national security affairs.

While secretary of state (1993–97), Warren Christopher frequently voiced his belief that "Iran will only change its behavior when the world makes it pay a sufficiently high political and economic price." So far the Administration has concluded that positive inducements such as trade and aid will not work. The United States seeks instead to deny Iran the military capabilities (by imposing strict export controls) and financial resources needed to carry out its policies. Washington has pledged to contain Iran unilaterally, if need be, although it has tried hard to persuade its allies to assist in this effort.

The United States maintains that it accepts the Iranian revolution and harbors no hostility to the Islamic religion. But it accuses Iran of supporting terrorism by inciting and funding groups violently opposed to Israel (including the Palestinian group Hamas and Hezbollah, the Lebanese Shiite militia) and assassinating Iranian dissidents abroad. In addition, the United States charges, Iran is trying to acquire weapons of mass destruction, is engaging in a buildup of conventional weapons, abuses human rights and opposes the Arab-Israeli peace process. Many Americans are appalled by the bounty placed on the head of writer Salmon Rushdie for alleged blasphemy against Islam. Washington claims that it is prepared to conduct a dialogue with authoritative representatives of Iran, but that Tehran has as yet shown no interest.

In March 1995, the United States toughened its policy toward Iran. The U.S. oil company Conoco had announced an agreement with Iran to develop two offshore oil fields in the Persian Gulf. U.S. companies were then purchasing one fifth of Iran's oil. While the deal was legal, it was an embarrassment to American diplomats who were seeking to persuade U.S. allies to reduce their trade with Iran. Stung by criticism from the Republicans, President Clinton prohibited the Conoco deal, and on May 6 he signed a sweeping order outlawing practically all trade with Iran. The embargo was strengthened in August 1996, when a new law imposed sanctions on foreign companies that invest more than $40 million (reduced to $20 million in August 1997) to help develop Iran's oil and gas fields. (A week after the President announced the tightening of the embargo, Turkey, a key U.S. ally, signed a $23 billion deal to purchase natural gas from Iran. The Administration subsequently determined that this does not violate the sanctions since the gas will originate in Turkmenistan.) Total's decision in September 1997 to defy U.S. sanctions and sign a major contract to develop the South Pars gas field in Iranian waters in the Persian Gulf put the Administration in a quandary. It did not want to start a trade war with its European allies and appeared to be seeking a way to avoid imposing the sanctions. Russia also warned the United States against interference.

American companies are increasingly resentful about being excluded from business in Iran and elsewhere. A coalition of 630 of the country's largest corporations formed an organization in April 1997 called USA Engage to oppose the imposition of unilateral U.S. trade sanctions abroad. U.S. oil companies are becoming more open about their desire to return to Iran; for example, in May 1997, Mobil, Amoco and Conoco attended a major energy conference in Isfahan, Iran.

Dealing with Iraq

Although the military defeat of Iraq in Desert Storm defused the immediate threat to the small Gulf states, the continued presence of Saddam Hussein compromises the region's long-term security. The United States aims to contain Baghdad by maintaining UN sanctions, by continued inspections and monitoring of Iraq's weapons programs by the UN Special Commission on Iraq (Unscom) and by enforcing no-fly zones in the north and south. As long as President Saddam Hussein remains in power in Iraq, there is little likelihood that the United States will let up its pressure. Secretary of State Madeleine K. Albright has said that if Saddam Hussein departs, the United States would quickly move to establish normal relations with a successor.

While prohibited by U.S. law from assassinating him, the U.S. Central Intelligence Agency (CIA) spent $100 million between 1991 and mid-1996 in an effort to oust the Iraqi president, according to *The Washington Post*. This included covert funding of two opposition groups formed in the wake of the war, the Iraqi National Congress and the Iraqi National Accord. The Iraqi invasion of the Kurdish zone in 1996 blew the cover on these operations and led to the death of a number of operatives. The United States does not want to get involved militarily in a civil war in the north and has tried to promote reconciliation among the two main Kurdish groups. It continues to provide humanitarian assistance to the people of northern Iraq through the UN and relief organizations.

An important question is how long the sanctions on Iraq will be maintained. U.S. policymakers strongly back their continuance, fearing that if they are lifted Saddam Hussein will quickly rearm and threaten his neighbors once again. Due to the hardships they have imposed on ordinary Iraqis, the governments of the UAE, Qatar and Oman favor ending them. The president of the UAE, Shaikh Zaid bin Sultan al-Nahayan, said in November 1997 that Saddam Hussein had made mistakes out of greed and should be forgiven. The sanctions have cost Turkey billions of dollars in lost trade and pipeline revenues, and it wants them ended. Many Americans, particularly those involved with humanitarian organizations, have also objected to the harm they are causing. Russia, France and China are all eager to exploit Iraqi oil resources once sanctions are lifted.

Assessing Dual Containment

So far dual containment has neither modified the behavior nor changed the government of Iran or Iraq. Most American experts on the Persian Gulf are convinced that the current policy is not working. According to former Secretary of State Henry A. Kissinger, "U.S. Gulf policy requires careful rethinking…we must either elevate 'dual containment' from a slogan into a strategy or define a strategy we are capable of implementing."

The U.S. trade embargo against Iran has been a unilateral effort, since Europe and Japan have not been willing to cooperate. The United States was gratified, however, when European countries suspended their "critical dialogue" with Iran (which admittedly produced meager results) in April 1997 after a German court implicated the Iranian leadership in the assassination of Iranian dissidents in Munich five years earlier. In the aftermath of the Khatami election, however, the "critical dialogue" may be resumed.

Some analysts argue that the Administration should maintain its tough stance against Iran: "The United States and Iran oppose each other because they understand each other all too well; it is the height of naïveté to think it's all just a 'failure of communication,'" according to Peter W. Rodman of the Nixon Center for Peace and Freedom. There has been no letup in congressional pressure, spearheaded by Senator Alfonse D'Amato (R-N.Y.), to be tough on Iran. House Speaker Newt Gingrich (R-Ga.) has called Iran "the most dangerous country in the world" and was instrumental in pushing through a bill in 1995 authorizing the spending of $20 million to destabilize the Tehran government.

Others note that the harshness of the policy the United States has adopted toward Iran is out of proportion to its policies toward countries such as China, North Korea and Vietnam with which it has serious and long-standing trade and security concerns. Overlooking human-rights abuses on the part of the Chinese government in order to do business and tolerating Chinese nuclear exports leave the Administration subject to charges of hypocrisy. As Joseph S. Nye Jr., then a senior U.S. Defense Department official stated, "if you treat China as an enemy, then you will have an enemy." The same rationale might be applied to Iran.

Dual containment, critics charge, offers no future vision for the region and no plan for a drawdown of U.S. forces. It is a purely military policy that forces the United States to be the policeman of the Gulf and postpones the time when the smaller Arab states come to terms with their two large neighbors. By seeking to exclude Iran and Iraq from Gulf affairs, the United States perpetuates an unnatural situation and prevents regional countries from working out their own security regime. If the governments in either Baghdad or Tehran were to fall, the policy of dual containment might become irrelevant, yet there is no successor policy.

Second Clinton Administration

The policies laid out in President Clinton's first term continued after his reelection, with many of the same officials in high policy positions. Secretary of State Albright, for example, had formerly dealt with Iraqi issues while U.S. representative to the UN. Martin Indyk, who played a major role in formulating the dual containment policy when he served on the National Security Council, is assistant secretary of state for Near Eastern affairs.

There were indications after the election of Iranian President Khatami that the Administration was quietly seeking to improve relations with Tehran. The United States was gratified by Khatami's moderate tone, and he made several cabinet changes that led to the removal of individuals Washington found objectionable. The new Iranian foreign minister, Kamal Kharrazi, indicated that Iran is now ready to resume ties if both states can find a way to do so. Iran was pleased when the Clinton Administration, despite its trade embargo on Iran, decided in July 1997 not to oppose construction of a $1.6 billion pipeline to carry gas from Turkmenistan through Iran to Turkey. Tehran was also happy when Washington put the Mojahedin, bitter opponents of the Iranian government who are based in Iraq, on its official list of terrorist organizations.

One important factor will be Israel's attitude; Israel encouraged Washington's hard-line approach to Iran during the first Clinton Administration. Israel and the United States have both pressured the Russian government not to assist Iran with its nuclear and missile programs, or allow Russian scientists and military institutes to do so. Significantly, both Israel and Saudi Arabia are reported to have urged Washington not to retaliate militarily should the Iranian government be proven to have had a role in the June 1996 truck bombing of the U.S. military housing complex in Dhahran in which 19 U.S. servicemen were killed.

Policies for the Future: the GCC

Formulation of a policy for the future must begin with a consideration of what U.S. interests in the Persian Gulf are and the factors likely to threaten these interests. The commitment of American forces assumes that the principal threat to the Gulf is external aggression. In the short term this may be true in regard to Iraq and possibly Iran. However, a strong case can be made that the primary threat to governments of the GCC countries in future years will be internal, not external. The real threats stem from the prospect of prolonged stagnation of oil prices, pressures for political reform and the resurgence of political Islam. The attacks on U.S. forces in Saudi Arabia may be harbingers of future challenges to the U.S. presence. If they are repeated, there may be a domestic debate over the wisdom of our continued commitment.

One option open to the United States is to exert greater pressure on the GCC leadership to make reforms. In other parts of the Middle East, the vehemence of the Islamic opposition seems directly correlated to the government's willingness to include it in the political process, which holds lessons for Bahrain and Saudi Arabia. Human rights is an issue Secretary Albright promises to make a priority, and this implies continued criticism of Iran as well as greater scrutiny of the Gulf monarchies. Excessive deference to friendly governments, such as in Riyadh, has led to a lack of information about the Saudi opposition that has hindered the investigation of the Dhahran bombing.

The United States now imports half its oil, as opposed to 36 percent at the time of the oil crisis in 1973. Protection of these imports remains the main rationale for the huge American commitment. Yet Persian Gulf oil is actually more important to other countries than it is to the United States. At present it accounts for about 20 percent of U.S. imports, 45 percent of Western Europe's and three quarters of Japan's. Protecting this oil is expensive, and some Americans complain that European and Japanese allies should not leave the United States to shoulder the burden alone.

The Administration also has encouraged the GCC states to purchase American arms. Between 1989 and 1996, the GCC states accounted for $40.6 billion out of the $80.5 billion in U.S.

REMEMBER WHEN THIS COUNTRY WAS GOING TO BE ENERGY INDEPENDENT? WHATEVER HAPPENED TO THAT IDEA?

IMPORTED OIL

CONTAINS NO LESS THAN 50% FOREIGN PETROLEUM

Ed Stein. Reprinted by permission of Newspaper Enterprise Associates, Inc.

arms sales to developing nations. In light of the budget difficulties these states are facing, and the criticism of such purchases by local dissidents, it may not be in the U.S. interest to push arms sales too strongly.

Iran

If the primary threat posed by Iran is its nuclear program, this could be addressed in the same manner as it was in North Korea, suggests Gary Sick, executive director of Gulf/2000, a research project on long-term trends in the Gulf based at Columbia University. In return for dismantling its older nuclear reactors, the United States agreed in 1994 to help provide North Korea with two safer light-water reactors and, until they were ready, to supply it with heavy fuel oil. (South Korea is to bear most of the cost.) The North Korean nuclear program is far more advanced than Iran's, which is still very small and years away from actual weapon production. As Sick points out, the proposed Iranian facilities are comparable to the plants to be provided to North Korea.

The first step to a more effective policy might be for Iranians and Americans to start talking to each other. The governments of the United States and Iran have become prisoners of their own rhetoric, often abetted by the news media. As Kissinger once said, "revenge is sweet, but it's not foreign policy." Even at the height of the cold war, the United States had an embassy in Moscow and carried on a dialogue on many subjects. Washington and Tehran need not start with the Gulf; they have much to discuss regarding neighboring regions, such as Afghanistan, Azerbaijan and the Caspian Sea. Until an official dialogue can begin, behind-the-scenes, "track two" discussions could take place. Confidence-building measures that have proven effective in other parts of the world appear long overdue for this region.

The President's cancellation of the Conoco deal and imposition of the embargo undercut moderate forces in Iran that had quietly sought rapprochement with the United States. In an interview with ABC news, former President Rafsanjani complained, "This was a message to the United States, which was not correctly understood." The Iranians could have chosen the French company Total for the deal from the beginning. Instead, they were trying to signal the Americans that, for the first time since the revolution, Iran was ready to do business again.

Generation Gap

The prerequisite to formulating effective policies is accurate information, which often is lacking in today's Gulf region. A new generation is coming to power in the Persian Gulf countries that is less likely than their parents to have been educated in or traveled to the West, or be sympathetic to its concerns. This is particularly serious in the case of Iran, where a whole generation has come of age without any personal knowledge of the country its government likes to refer to as "the Great Satan," and very few Americans have visited Iran for almost 20 years. In 1978 there were some 100,000 Iranians studying abroad, half in the United States. In 1995–96, only 2,600 Iranians were studying here (as opposed to 4,200 students from Saudi Arabia). There appears to be an increasing risk that a new generation of Iranians will simply lose interest in the United States and blame it for trying to prevent them from developing their country.

America's understanding of Iraq is even more limited than its knowledge of Iran. For most of the past four decades, the two countries have been estranged: relations were severed from 1967 to 1984 and again from 1990 until the present. In Saudi Arabia, many senior princes in the past were educated in the United States, but the trend now is increasingly to study at domestic institutions. Saudi Arabia's top cleric, Shaikh Abdul Aziz bin Baz, recently warned that travel to the West could corrupt young Muslims. All this has contributed to a dangerous information gap between policymakers in the Persian Gulf countries and the United States.

Critics have suggested that instead of a policy of containment and punishment, the United States could provide these states with incentives for better relations. An economic component might be added to complement dual containment's military focus. U.S. companies could be allowed to do business with Iran and the moderate forces there cultivated. Instead of dual containment, the United States could pursue a policy of dual engagement.

◆§

The American age in the Persian Gulf, historically speaking, has just begun and will probably be of much shorter duration than that of the British. While it lasts, the United States should work to promote regional reconciliation and not permit the countries to postpone facing their problems. It is time for the United States to formulate policies for the long term.

Talking It Over

A Note for Students and Discussion Groups

This issue of the HEADLINE SERIES, like its predecessors, is published for every serious reader, specialized or not, who takes an interest in the subject. Many of our readers will be in classrooms, seminars or community discussion groups. Particularly with them in mind, we present below some discussion questions—suggested as a starting point only—and references for further reading.

Discussion Questions

What were some of the internal changes set in motion in the Persian Gulf states after the discovery of oil? Why is having oil a curse as well as a blessing?

How would you assess the relative importance of the factors (such as Islam, tribalism, nationalism, pan-Arabism, oil economics, democracy/civil society movement, women's rights, foreign ties) that are likely to influence Gulf states and societies in the next decade, as they try to reconcile continuity and change?

The principal U.S. interest in the Gulf is the unhindered export of its oil. But what other interests does the United States have there, and what actions should it take to secure them?

Should human-rights abuses or the denial of political participation be a priority?

What has happened to the "new world order" proclaimed by President Bush at the time of the Persian Gulf war? Then, the Soviet Union, along with many European and Arab countries, supported U.S. aims, and the UN played a key role in ending the conflict. How has the international scene changed since the early 1990's? Do you think the United States could assemble another such coalition today?

Seven years after Desert Storm, Saddam Hussein remains in power and there is a sense of unfinished business in the Persian Gulf. How do you regard the legacy of the war—its positive and negative aspects for the United States and regional states?

The United States encouraged the Kurds to rebel after Desert Storm, yet when they did so, it did not stop their repression by the Baghdad government. What responsibility does the United States have to the Kurds? Should they be entitled to their own state? How can the United States ease their plight in northern Iraq?

Since the Iranian revolution of 1978–79 and the taking of American hostages there, the United States and Iran have been at loggerheads. Yet this stands as an exception to the close ties the two countries maintained throughout most of the twentieth century. The United States has restored relations with former enemies such as China and Vietnam. Under what conditions should it do so with Iran?

Annotated Reading List

Brzezinski, Zbigniew, Scowcroft, Brent, and Murphy, Richard, "Differentiated Containment." *Foreign Affairs*, May/June 1997. Three former high-level officials criticize the strategy of "dual containment" and call for a more nuanced approach.

"Children of the Islamic Revolution: A Survey of Iran." *The Economist* (London), January 18, 1997. An excellent overview of contemporary Iran.

Cottrell, Alvin J., ed., *The Persian Gulf States: A General Survey*. Baltimore, MD,

The Johns Hopkins University Press, 1980. Still the best one-volume reference to the Persian Gulf, especially strong on history and society.

Dekmejian, R. Hrair, "The Rise of Political Islamism in Saudi Arabia." *The Middle East Journal*, Autumn 1994. An insightful profile of the Islamic opposition and the regime's response.

Gause, F. Gregory, III, "The Gulf Conundrum: Economic Change, Population Growth, and Political Stability in the GCC States." *The Washington Quarterly*, Winter 1997. Political scientist explains the dilemmas now facing the Gulf monarchies.

Gordon, Michael R., and Trainor, Bernard E., *The Generals' War: The Inside Story of the Conflict in the Gulf*. Boston, MA, Little, Brown, 1995. A thorough behind-the-scenes account.

Human Rights Watch/Middle East, *Routine Abuse, Routine Denial: Civil Rights and the Political Crisis in Bahrain*. New York, Human Rights Watch, July 1997. Describes the origins of the continuing unrest in Bahrain and criticizes the government's human-rights violations.

Izady, Mehrdad R., *The Kurds: A Concise Handbook*. Washington, DC, Taylor & Francis, 1992. The best one-volume introduction to the subject.

Marr, Phebe, *The Modern History of Iraq*. Boulder, CO, Westview Press, 1985. Expert examines the political, economic and social transformations that have created modern Iraq.

Metz, Helen Chapin, ed., *Persian Gulf States: Country Studies*, 3rd ed. Washington, DC, Library of Congress, Federal Research Division (Area Handbook series), 1994. Very useful compendium of information on the Gulf monarchies; see the companion volumes on Iran (1989), Iraq (1990) and Saudi Arabia (1993).

Milani, Mohsen M., *The Making of Iran's Islamic Revolution: From Monarchy to Islamic Republic*, 2nd ed. Boulder, CO, Westview Press, 1994. This study by a political scientist considers the preconditions for revolution under the Pahlavi dynasty (1925–79) and analyzes factional politics in post-Khomeini Iran.

Munif, Abdelrahman, *Cities of Salt*, trans. Peter Theroux. New York, Vintage Books, 1989. A novel set in Saudi Arabia sensitively chronicles the profound changes caused by the discovery of oil.

Sick, Gary G., and Potter, Lawrence G., eds., *The Persian Gulf at the Millennium: Essays in Politics, Economy, Security, and Religion*. New York, St. Martin's Press, 1997. Prominent experts identify issues likely to affect the region in the future, including rapid demographic change, uncertain oil prices, stagnant economies, the resurgence of political Islam and heavy defense spending.

Zanoyan, Vahan, "After the Oil Boom: The Holiday Ends in the Gulf." *Foreign Affairs*, Nov./Dec. 1995. Oil economist warns that the greatest risk to U.S. interests in the Persian Gulf is monarchs who refuse to make political and economic reforms.